Mind and Language

Mind and Language

WOLFSON COLLEGE LECTURES 1974

EDITED BY
SAMUEL GUTTENPLAN

CLARENDON PRESS · OXFORD

Oxford University Press, Walton Street, Oxford OX2 6DP

OXFORD LONDON GLASGOW NEW YORK TORONTO MELBOURNE WELLINGTON
CAPE TOWN IBADAN NAIROBI DAR ES SALAAM LUSAKA ADDIS ABABA
DELHI BOMBAY CALCUTTA MADRAS KARACHI
KUALA LUMPUR SINGAPORE JAKARTA HONG KONG TOKYO

First published 1975
Reprinted 1977

British Library Cataloguing in Publication Data
Mind and language. – (Wolfson College. Lectures; 1974)
   1. Thought and thinking – Philosophy 2. Languages – Philosophy
   3. Language – Psychology I. Guttenplan, Samuel II. Series
   128'.2   BF455   77–30421
   ISBN 0–19–875043–9

Printed in Great Britain
by Richard Clay (The Chaucer Press), Ltd.,
Bungay, Suffolk

for
SIR ISAIAH BERLIN, O.M.
President of Wolfson College 1966–1975

Preface

THE essays in this collection began life as the Wolfson College Lectures for 1974. These lectures, under the title 'Mind and Language', were delivered at the University of Oxford in Hilary term 1974; they are printed here in the order in which they were given. However, there are many variations between the spoken and printed versions of each of these essays. Most of the authors include material here which they did not have time to develop in their lectures but the contributions of W. V. Quine and Michael Dummett are very much longer than the originals and some comment should be made about this. Of the two essays printed here 'The Nature of Natural Knowledge' was Quine's Wolfson lecture but he allowed me to print 'Mind and Verbal Dispositions' and this is an illuminating companion to his lecture. The Appendix to Michael Dummett's essay developed from a seminar which he gave with Donald Davidson in the term following that of the lecture series and should help to locate more precisely the bases of his disagreement with the Davidsonian programme.

I had considerable help in organizing the original lecture series and would like to thank Professor Dana Scott and Mr. Henry Hardy for this. Thanks are due too to Mrs. Beryl Schweder for her secretarial assistance with the lecture series.

SAMUEL GUTTENPLAN

Oxford

Contents

Introduction

S. D. GUTTENPLAN

WHETHER as general questions about the relationship between the so-called 'propositional attitudes' and linguistic meaning, or as more specific questions about the connections between certain mental and linguistic concepts, issues of mind and language bulk large in current philosophical literature. In fact, of all issues, one would be justified in labelling these as perhaps most characteristic of philosophy in our time. Yet even a superficial survey of philosophical works since at least the late seventeenth century would show that concern with these questions is not merely a phenomenon of this century. This is not because one can find one or two writers here and there before the beginning of our century who tried to detail the relationship between mind and language. It is because one finds developed attempts by many writers to solve the very sorts of problems which we recognize as so characteristically modern; and, in the eighteenth century, these attempts were loosely organized around a particular theme. Of course, current work on mind–language questions owes almost nothing to these early investigations; though, to a surprising degree, the general form of question is shared. None the less, one way of appreciating the common background of the essays in this volume is by understanding why they owe so little to the tradition which posed many of the questions they consider. What follows is a very brief sketch, by way of example, of the eighteenth-century treatment of these questions together with some discussion of how the basic contributions of the last hundred years have made this treatment appear unfruitful. Though there are doubtless more direct ways of introducing the subject matter of this book, none can show, in quite the way that this approach can, the sort of progress which has been made in dealing with this kind of philosophical question; progress which forces us to view much

2   S. D. Guttenplan

previous work as irrelevant or superficial, and which gives contemporary philosophy of language and mind that characteristic appearance of self-containment.

Locke, after devoting many pages of the *Essay* to detailing the impediments with which language encumbers the attainment of knowledge, felt it necessary to explain why he blamed language and not, more simply, the users of languages:

... [when] I began to examine the extent and certainty of our knowledge, I found it had so near a connexion with words that, unless their force and manner of signification were first well observed, there could be very little said clearly and pertinently concerning knowledge ... [words] interpose themselves so much between our understandings and the truth which it would contemplate and apprehend that, like the *medium* through which visible objects pass, their obscurity and disorder does not seldom cast a mist before our eyes and impose upon our understandings.[1]

Though Locke's description of the 'imperfections' of language and his account of the consequences of these imperfections for human understanding do not appear profound, these parts of the *Essay* were the major source of eighteenth-century interest in the philosophy of language and mind. The preoccupation—for that is what it was—of these writers was with the question: what was the origin of human language; and the question, if not some of the answers to it, was prompted by Locke's *Essay*. By pointing out the connection between language and knowledge, Locke made the understanding of language a prerequisite for fixing the boundaries of knowledge. The idea that language could be understood by discovering its origins comes partly from the 'plain, historical method' tone of the *Essay* and partly from Locke's conjecture about such origins at the beginning of Book III. Condillac, Mandeville, Adam Smith, Rousseau, James Harris, Maupertuis, Turgot, and Monboddo, among many others, speculated about this subject and most of them believed that, in trying to uncover the origin of language, they were investigating its nature. It seemed to them, and can without reflection seem to us, that language as a human activity must have had 'origins' in the way that, say, chess did and that, however cloudy, these beginnings should be traceable. Further, there was the hope that the discovery or reconstruction of these origins would help in deciding the role of language in the exercise of human intellectual capacities.

From our vantage-point the many attempts to reconstruct the

[1] *An Essay Concerning Human Understanding*, Book III, Chap. IX, ¶ 21.

natural history of language and mind may seem so speculative as to be little more than curiosities in the history of linguistics; one may be disinclined to allow them as in any way philosophical. My suggestion, however, is that they should be seen as part of the prehistory of contemporary philosophy of language. The interesting question is why they now seem so empty.

A first attempt at explanation, and one which can be fairly quickly dismissed, is this: theories about the origins of language were vain attempts to apply the then only partially understood scientific method to a complex question. The present unimportance of such theories lies in their failure to come to any defensible conclusions. Of course, it is true that theories of origins have not advanced our knowledge about languages and, therefore, about minds. Still, it would not follow from this that such theories are completely misguided and deserve no consideration. Perhaps, a defender of such theories could argue, the problem was and is the simple unavailability of empirical data; the project is worthwhile, but the historical record is too meagre to allow any hope of success.

Such an explanation, though, will not do. The reason why no serious contemporary thinker would undertake an empirical investigation into the natural history of language as an aid in language–mind issues goes much deeper. Briefly it is this: the very posing of certain questions about the origins of human language presupposes a conceptual gap between mental and linguistic notions, and we have come to believe that such a presupposition is incoherent. There is a perfectly clear sense in which one might ask: how did language begin? The answer would be given in terms of evolutionary mechanisms not yet formulable in any detail. What creates the incoherence in the particular form of question put in the eighteenth century is that it begins with men already highly developed intellectually and asks: how did language get started among these creatures? The assumption behind most inquiries into the origins of language was that language was a product of thought; a mirror reflecting, however obscurely, our mental processes. Even those, like Locke, who gave language an active role in the determination of thought would have insisted on the possibility of characterizing a language without reference to mental concepts and mental concepts without reference to a language. Locke's efforts to catalogue the allegedly deleterious effects of language on human understanding clearly reveal his belief in such separability.

This view of the relationship between language and thought did not

4 S. D. Guttenplan

go unchallenged. Vico, Hamann, Herder, and others reacted vehe-mently against the Enlightenment and attacked attempts at sharp distinction between language and thought. In characteristically emphatic fashion, Hamann wrote: 'Even if I were as eloquent as Demosthenes, I would merely have to repeat a single maxim three times: reason is language, λογος. This is the bone I gnaw on and on it I will gnaw myself to death.'[1] And Herder's scathing description of Condillac's explanation of the genesis of language between two children alone together in a desert includes this observation:

> His two children are thrown together without any knowledge of signs and—lo and behold!—they communicate from the first moment. And simply by means of this communication they first learn 'to associate thoughts with the outcry of feeling which is the natural sign of feeling'. Learning natural signs of feeling by communication? Learning in the same way which thoughts are associated with them? . . . I cannot comprehend any of this.[2]

My aim, however, is not to contrast contemporary philosophy of language with all eighteenth-century theories but just with those which shared the presupposition that the origin of language among languageless but otherwise human creatures could be traced.

In the present century, largely as a result of Frege's work, philoso-phical theories of language, however diverse, tend to agree in holding that some of the concepts which are necessary to describe language are also an integral part of the description of mental states and attitudes.[3] Thus in a very important sense mind and language cannot be separated, though this is not quite to say, as Hamann did, that language and thought are one. To ask how language began while assuming that human beings had, by and large, the same thoughts and feelings before and after the acquisition of language is to ask a question which is unanswerable because it is based on conceptual confusion. The origin theories of the eighteenth century, involving a conception of the mind as almost literally containing ideas which could be labelled, more or less tidily, by means of words, reveal just

---

[1] Cited in Ernst Cassirer's *Philosophy of Symbolic Forms*, Vol. I, New Haven: Yale Univ. Press, 1953.

[2] *Abhandlung über den Ursprung der Sprache*, 1772, Part I, Section 1.

[3] One of the best-known features of Frege's philosophy of logic and language was his thoroughgoing anti-psychologism, and it might appear that in crediting Frege with connecting language and thought this feature is being ignored. How-ever, so long as one is clear about the non-psychological character of Frege's notion of sense and about the dependence of ascriptions of belief on that notion, there is nothing above which is inconsistent with anti-psychologism.

such confusion. To be fair, it was during that century that even the most rationalistic thinkers began to recognize that such 'labels' could have a significant effect on the 'availability' of the items labelled. None the less, real advance in thinking about language and its connection to mind was possible only when the conceptual interlocking between the two areas was understood. One caveat is necessary here. In using terms such as 'mental' and 'thought' to describe both contemporary and eighteenth-century approaches to language I am in no way trying to suggest that these concepts have remained the same. On the contrary, they have undergone change precisely because of changed attitudes about the connection between mind and language. My point is that, whether one prefers to talk of dispositions or of mental processes, the real *locus* of progress in language–mind issues is in the realization that concepts needed to describe the one are part of the description of the other.

But what are these concepts which unite our attempts to understand language and mind? It is tempting to say no more than that the answer to this is contained at least in part in the essays which follow. However, a very general answer, and one which might prove helpful in appreciating these essays, can be given by considering the concept of truth in Frege's philosophy of language. It is Frege's work which provides much of the background to the philosophy of language–mind questions in this century, and the debt of each of the authors in this volume to that work should be obvious. This is not to say that there are no radical departures from Frege's theories either in or out of this volume. It is just that his theories have acted both as an inspiration to some and as a target of criticism to others (these groups being not necessarily mutually exclusive), so that, whatever one's views, those of Frege have had a role in their formation. If one wants to grasp a particular proposal in the philosophy of language, one cannot do better than to discover how that proposal is related to the Fregean conception of language.

The appeal of Frege's view lies in his use of the concept of truth both to explicate the notion of linguistic meaning and to connect the latter with the concepts of judgement, assertion, and belief—various propositional attitudes. The core of his theory can be roughly characterized by the following maxims: (1) any theory of language should show that the meanings of individual words are given by their contributions to the meaning of sentences in the language. (2) The meanings of sentences can be grasped by recognizing the conditions under which the sentences are true. Indeed, for Frege, the sense of a sentence is that which, together with extra-linguistic facts, determines the truth value of a sentence. (3) The assigning of senses to words and sentences is required in the attribution of propositional attitudes such as belief, knowledge, and assertion to speakers of the language.

In the last seventy-five years we have seen many theories which seek to challenge Frege's: those which would replace the notion of truth by one of verification; theories which question the abstractness of 'truth' and would substitute 'assent-conditions';[1] theories which retain the basic insight but use developments in formal logic (such as Tarski's truth definition), thereby avoiding Frege's commitment to senses and truth values as Platonic entities;[2] and, finally, theories which in various ways attempt to achieve yet finer analyses by defining meaning, and hence truth, in terms of, it is claimed, more fundamental concepts.[3] In addition, there are views of language whose debt to Frege is essentially negative; views which, using Frege's theory as an example, challenge the idea that truth, verification, or any *one* notion is the key to understanding meaning.[4] Of course, both the above description of Frege's view and the outline of theories which are related to it require myriad qualifications. My hope is that the essays which follow will enable the reader to formulate these for himself.

[1] Cf. W. V. Quine, *Word and Object*, Cambridge, Mass.: M.I.T. Press, 1960.
[2] Cf. D. Davidson, 'Truth and Meaning', *Synthese* (1967).
[3] Cf. H. P. Grice, 'Meaning', *Philosophical Review* (1957), and P. F. Strawson, *Meaning and Truth*, Inaugural lecture, Oxford: O.U.P., 1970.
[4] Cf. L. Wittgenstein, *Philosophical Investigations*, Oxford: Basil Blackwell, 1953.

1 *Thought and Talk*

D. DAVIDSON

WHAT is the connection between thought and language? The dependence of speaking on thinking is evident, for to speak is to express thoughts. This dependence is manifest in endless further ways. Someone who utters the sentence 'The candle is out' as a sentence of English must intend to utter words that are true if and only if an indicated candle is out at the time of utterance, and he must believe that by making the sounds he does he is uttering words that are true only under those circumstances. These intentions and beliefs are not apt to be dwelt on by the fluent speaker. But though they may not normally command attention, their absence would be enough to show he was not speaking English, and the absence of any analogous thoughts would show he was not speaking at all.

The issue is on the other side: can there be thought without speech? A first and natural reaction is that there can be. There is the familiar, irksome experience of not being able to find the words to express one's ideas. On occasion one may decide that the editorial writer has put a point better than one could oneself. And there is Norman Malcolm's dog who, having chased a squirrel into the woods, barks up the wrong tree. It is hard not to credit the dog with the belief that the squirrel is in that tree.

A definite, if feebler, intuition tilts the other way. It is possible to wonder whether the speaker who can't find the right words has a clear idea. Attributions of intentions and beliefs to dogs smack of anthropomorphism. A primitive behaviourism, baffled by the privacy of unspoken thoughts, may take comfort in the view that thinking is really 'talking to oneself'—silent speech.

Beneath the surface of these opposed tendencies run strong, if turgid, currents, which may help to explain why philosophers have, for the most part, preferred taking a stand on the issue to producing an argument. Whatever the reason, the question of the relationship between thought and speech seems seldom to have been asked for its own sake. The usual assumption is that one or the other, speech or thought, is by comparison easy to understand, and therefore the more obscure one (whichever that is) may be illuminated by analysing or explaining it in terms of the other.

The assumption is, I think, false: neither language nor thinking can be fully explained in terms of the other, and neither has conceptual priority. The two are, indeed, linked, in the sense that each requires the other in order to be understood; but the linkage is not so complete that either suffices, even when reasonably reinforced, to explicate the other. To make good this claim what is chiefly needed is to show how thought depends on speech, and this is the thesis I want to refine, and then to argue for.

We attribute a thought to a creature whenever we assertively employ a positive sentence the main verb of which is psychological—in English, 'believes', 'knows', 'hopes', 'desires', 'thinks', 'fears', 'is interested' are examples—followed by a sentence and preceded by the name or description of the creature. (A 'that' may optionally or necessarily follow the verb.) Some such sentences attribute states, others report events or processes: 'believes', 'thinks', and 'wants' report states, while 'came to believe', 'forgot', 'concluded', 'noticed', 'is proving' report events or processes. Sentences that can be used to attribute a thought exhibit what is often called, or analysed as, semantic intensionality, which means that the attribution may be changed from true to false, or false to true, by substitutions in the contained sentences that would not alter the truth value of that sentence in isolation.

I do not take for granted that if a creature has a thought, then we can, with resources of the kind just sketched, correctly attribute that thought to him. But thoughts so attributable at least constitute a good sample of the totality.

It is doubtful whether the various sorts of thought can be reduced to one, or even to a few: desire, knowledge, belief, fear, interest, to name some important cases, are probably logically independent to the extent that none can be defined using the others, even along with such further notions as truth and cause. Nevertheless, belief is central to all kinds of thought. If someone is glad that, or notices that, or remembers that, or knows that, the gun is loaded, then he must believe that the gun is loaded. Even to wonder whether the gun is loaded, or to speculate on the possibility that the gun is loaded, requires the belief, for example, that a gun is a weapon, that it is a more or less enduring physical object, and so on. There are good reasons for not insisting on any particular list of beliefs that are needed if a creature is to wonder whether a gun is loaded. Nevertheless, it is necessary that there be endless interlocked beliefs. The system of such beliefs identifies a thought by locating it in a logical and epistemic space.

Having a thought requires that there be a background of beliefs, but having a particular thought does not depend on the state of belief with respect to that very thought. If I consider going to a certain concert, I know I will be put to a degree of trouble and expense, and I have more complicated beliefs about the enjoyment I will experience. I will enjoy hearing Beethoven's Grosse Fuge, say, but only provided the performance achieves a reasonable standard, and I am able to remain attentive. I have the thought of going to the concert, but until I decide whether to go, I have no fixed belief that I will go; until that time, I merely entertain the thought.

We may say, summarizing the last two paragraphs, that a thought is defined by a system of beliefs, but is itself autonomous with respect to belief.

We usually think that having a language consists largely in being able to speak, but in what follows speaking will play only an indirect part. What is essential to my argument is the idea of an interpreter, someone who understands the utterances of another. The considerations to be put forward imply, I think, that a speaker must himself be an interpreter of others, but I shall not try to demonstrate that an interpreter must be a speaker, though there may be good reason to hold this. Perhaps it is worth pointing out that the notion of a language, or of two people speaking the same language does not seem to be needed here. Two speakers could interpret each other's utterances without there being, in any ordinary sense, a common language. (I do not want to deny that in other contexts the notion of a shared language may be very important.)

The chief thesis of this paper is that a creature cannot have thoughts unless it is an interpreter of the speech of another. This thesis does not imply the possibility of reduction, behaviouristic or otherwise, of thoughts to speech; indeed the thesis imputes no priority to language, epistemological or conceptual. The claim also falls short of similar claims in that it allows that there may be thoughts for which the speaker cannot find words, or for which there are no words.

Someone who can interpret an utterance of the English sentence 'The gun is loaded' must have many beliefs, and these beliefs must be much like the beliefs someone must have if he entertains the thought that the gun is loaded. The interpreter must, we may suppose, believe that a gun is a weapon, and that it is a more or less enduring physical object. There is probably no definite list of things that must be believed by someone who understands the sentence 'The gun is loaded,' but it is necessary that there be endless interlocked beliefs.

An interpreter knows the conditions under which utterances of sentences are true, and often knows that if certain sentences are true, others must be. For example, an interpreter of English knows that if 'The gun is loaded and the door is locked' is true, then 'The door is locked' is true. The sentences of a language have a location in the logical space created by the pattern of such relationships. Obviously the pattern of relations between sentences is very much like the pattern of relations between thoughts. This fact has encouraged the view that it is redundant to take both patterns as basic. If thoughts are primary, a language seems to serve no purpose but to express or convey thoughts; while if we take speech as primary, it is tempting to analyse thoughts as speech dispositions: as Sellars puts it, '. . . thinking at the distinctly human level . . . is essentially verbal activity'.[1] But clearly the parallel between the structure of thoughts and the structure of sentences provides no argument for the primacy of either, and only a presumption in favour of their interdependence.

We have been talking freely of thoughts, beliefs, meanings, and interpretations; or rather, freely using sentences that contain these words. But of course it is not clear what entities, or sorts of entities, there must be to make systematic sense of such sentences. However, talk apparently of thoughts and sayings does belong to a familiar mode of explanation of human behaviour and must be considered an organized department of common sense that may as well be called a theory. One way of examining the relation between thought and language is by inspecting the theory implicit in this sort of explanation.

[1] Wilfrid Sellars, 'Conceptual Change', in *Conceptual Change*, ed. G. Pearce and P. Maynard, Dordrecht, 1973, p. 82.

Part of the theory deals with the teleological explanation of action. We wonder why a man raises his arm; an explanation might be that he wanted to attract the attention of a friend. This explanation would fail if the arm-raiser didn't believe that by raising his arm he would attract the attention of his friend, so the complete explanation of his raising his arm, or at any rate a more complete explanation, is that he wanted to attract the attention of his friend *and* believed that by raising his arm he would attract his friend's attention. Explanation of this familiar kind has some features worth emphasizing. It explains what is relatively apparent—an arm-raising—by appeal to factors that are far more problematical: desires and beliefs. But if we were to ask for evidence that the explanation is correct, this evidence would in the end consist of more data concerning the sort of event being explained, namely further behaviour which is explained by the postulated beliefs and desires. Adverting to beliefs and desires to explain action is therefore a way of fitting an action into a pattern of behaviour made coherent by the theory. This does not mean, of course, that beliefs are nothing but patterns of behaviour, or that the relevant patterns can be defined without using the concepts of belief and desire. Nevertheless, there is a clear sense in which attributions of belief and desire, and hence teleological explanations of belief and desire, are supervenient on behaviour more broadly described.

A characteristic of teleological explanation not shared by explanation generally is the way in which it appeals to the concept of *reason*. The belief and desire that explain an action must be such that anyone who had that belief and desire would have a reason to act in that way. What's more, the descriptions we provide of desire and belief must, in teleological explanation, exhibit the rationality of the action in the light of the content of the belief and the object of the desire.

The cogency of a teleological explanation rests, as remarked, on its ability to discover a coherent pattern in the behaviour of an agent. Coherence here includes the idea of rationality both in the sense that the action to be explained must be reasonable in the light of the assigned desires and beliefs, but also in the sense that the assigned desires and beliefs must fit with one another. The methodological presumption of rationality does not make it impossible to attribute irrational thoughts and actions to an agent, but it does impose a burden on such attributions. We weaken the intelligibility of attributions of thoughts of any kind to the extent that we fail to uncover a consistent pattern of beliefs and, finally, of actions, for it is only against a background of such a pattern that we can identify thoughts. If we see a man pulling on both ends of a piece of string, we may decide he is fighting against himself, that he wants to move the string in incompatible directions. Such an explanation would require elaborate backing. No problem arises if the explanation is that he wants to break the string.

From the point of view of someone giving teleological explanations of the actions of another, it clearly makes no sense to assign priority either to desires or to beliefs. Both are essential to the explanation of behaviour, and neither is more directly open to observation than the other. This creates a problem, for it means that behaviour, which is the main evidential basis for attributions of belief and desire, is reckoned the result of two forces less open to public observation. Thus where one constellation of beliefs and desires will rationalize an action, it is always possible to find a quite different constellation that will do as well. Even a generous sample of actions threatens to leave open an unacceptably large number of alternative explanations.

Fortunately a more refined theory is available, one still firmly based on common sense: the theory of preference, or decision-making, under uncertainty. The theory was first made precise by Frank Ramsey, though he viewed it as a matter of providing a foundation for the concept of probability rather than as a piece of philosophical psychology.[1] Ramsey's theory works by quantifying strength of preference and degree of belief in such a way as to make sense of the natural idea that in choosing a course of action we consider not only how desirable various outcomes are, but also how apt available courses of action are to produce those outcomes. The theory does not assume that we can judge degrees of belief or make numerical comparisons of value directly. Rather it postulates a reasonable pattern of preferences between courses of action, and shows how to construct a system of quantified beliefs and desires to explain the choices. Given the idealized conditions postulated by the theory, Ramsey's method makes it possible to identify the relevant beliefs and desires uniquely. Instead of talking of postulation, we might put the matter this way: to the extent that we can see the actions of an agent as falling into a consistent (rational) pattern of a certain sort, we can explain those actions in terms of a system of quantified beliefs and desires.

[1] Frank Ramsey, 'Truth and Probability', in *Foundations of Mathematics and Other Essays*, ed. R. B. Braithwaite, London, 1931.

We shall come back to decision theory presently; now it is time to turn to the question of how speech is interpreted. The immediate aim of a theory of interpretation is to give the meaning of an arbitrary utterance by a member of a language community. Central to interpretation, I have argued, is a theory of truth that satisfies Tarski's Convention T (modified in certain ways to apply to a natural language). Such a theory yields, for every utterance of every sentence of the language, a theorem of the form: 'An utterance of sentence *s* by a speaker *x* at time *t* is true if and only if ——.' Here '*s*' is to be replaced by a description of a sentence, and the blank by a statement of the conditions under which an utterance of the sentence is true relative to the parameters of speaker and time. In order to interpret a particular utterance it is neither necessary nor sufficient to know the entire theory: it is enough to know what the theory says the truth conditions are for the utterance, and to know that those conditions are entailed by a theory of the required sort. On the other hand, to belong to a speech community—to be an interpreter of the speech of others—one does need to know much of a whole theory, in effect, and to know that it is a theory of the right kind.[1]

A theory of interpretation, like a theory of action, allows us to redescribe certain events in a revealing way. Just as a theory of action can answer the question of what an agent is doing when he has raised his arm by redescribing the act as one of trying to catch his friend's attention, so a method of interpretation can lead to redescribing the utterance of certain sounds as an act of saying that snow is white. At this point, however, the analogy breaks down. For decision theory can also explain actions, while it is not at all clear how a theory of interpretation can explain a speaker's uttering the words 'Snow is white.' But this is, after all, to be expected, for uttering words is an action, and so must draw for its teleological explanation on beliefs and desires. Interpretation is not irrelevant to the teleological explanation of speech, since to explain why someone said something we need to know, among other things, his own interpretation of what he said, that is, what he believes his words mean in the circumstances under which he speaks. Naturally this will involve some of his beliefs about how others will interpret his words.

The interlocking of the theory of action with interpretation will emerge in another way if we ask how a method of interpretation is

[1] There is further discussion of these issues in my 'Radical Interpretation', *Dialectica* (Vol. 27, Nos. 3–4, 1973).

tested. In the end, the answer must be that it helps bring order into our understanding of behaviour. But at an intermediary stage, we can see that the attitude of *holding true* or *accepting as true*, as directed towards sentences, must play a central role in giving form to a theory. On the one hand, most uses of language tell us directly, or shed light on the question, whether a speaker holds a sentence to be true. If a speaker's purpose is to give information, or to make an honest assertion, then normally the speaker believes he is uttering a sentence true under the circumstances. If he utters a command, we may usually take this as showing that he holds a certain sentence (closely related to the sentence uttered) to be false; similarly for many cases of deceit. When a question is asked, it generally indicates that the questioner does not know whether a certain sentence is true; and so on. In order to infer from such evidence that a speaker holds a sentence true we need to know much about his desires and beliefs, but we do not have to know what his words mean.

On the other hand, knowledge of the circumstances under which someone holds sentences true is central to interpretation. We saw in the case of thoughts that although most thoughts are not beliefs, it is the pattern of belief that allows us to identify any thought; analogously, in the case of language, although most utterances are not concerned with truth, it is the pattern of sentences held true that gives sentences their meaning.

The attitude of holding a sentence to be true (under specified conditions) relates belief and interpretation in a fundamental way. We can know that a speaker holds a sentence to be true without knowing what he means by it or what belief it expresses for him. But if we know he holds the sentence true *and* we know how to interpret it, then we can make a correct attribution of belief. Symmetrically, if we know what belief a sentence held true expresses, we know how to interpret it. The methodological problem of interpretation is to see how, given the sentences a man accepts as true under given circumstances, to work out what his beliefs are and what his words mean. The situation is again similar to the situation in decision theory where, given a man's preferences between alternative courses of action, we can discern both his beliefs and his desires. Of course it should not be thought that a theory of interpretation will stand alone, for as we noticed, there is no chance of telling when a sentence is held true without being able to attribute desires and being able to describe actions as having complex intentions. This observation does not deprive the theory of interpretation of interest, but assigns it a place within a more comprehensive theory of action and thought.[1]

It is still unclear whether interpretation is required for a theory of action, which is the question we set ourselves to answer. What is certain is that all the standard ways of testing theories of decision or preference under uncertainty rely on the use of language. It is relatively simple to eliminate the necessity for verbal responses on the part of the subject: he can be taken to have expressed a preference by taking action, by moving directly to achieve his end, rather than by saying what he wants. But this cannot settle the question of what he has chosen. A man who takes an apple rather than a pear when offered both may be expressing a preference for what is on his left rather than his right, what is red rather than yellow, what is seen first, or judged more expensive. Repeated tests may make some readings of his actions more plausible than others, but the problem will remain how to tell what he judges to be a repetition of the same alternative. Tests that involve uncertain events—choices between gambles—are even harder to present without using words. The psychologist, sceptical of his ability to be certain how a subject is interpreting his instructions, must add a theory of verbal interpretation to the theory to be tested. If we think of all choices as revealing a preference that one sentence rather than another be true, the resulting total theory should provide an interpretation of sentences, and at the same time assign beliefs and desires, both of the latter conceived as relating the agent to sentences or utterances. This composite theory would explain all behaviour, verbal and otherwise.

All this strongly suggests that the attribution of desires and beliefs (and other thoughts) must go hand in hand with the interpretation of speech, that neither the theory of decision nor of interpretation can be successfully developed without the other. But it remains to say, in more convincing detail, why the attribution of thought depends on the interpretation of speech. The general, and not very informative, reason is that without speech we cannot make the fine distinctions between thoughts that are essential to the explanations we can sometimes confidently supply. Our manner of attributing attitudes ensures that all the expressive power of language can be used to make such

---

[1] The interlocking of decision theory and radical interpretation is explored also in my 'Psychology as Philosophy', in *Philosophy of Psychology*, ed. S. C. Brown, London, 1974, pp. 41–52; and in my 'Belief and the Basis of Meaning', *Synthese* (vol. 27, 1974, pp. 309–24).

distinctions. One can believe that Scott is not the author of *Waverley* while not doubting that Scott is Scott; one can want to be the discoverer of a creature with a heart without wanting to be the discoverer of a creature with a kidney. One can intend to bite into the apple in the hand without intending to bite into the only apple with a worm in it; and so forth. The intensionality we make so much of in the attribution of thoughts is very hard to make much of when speech is not present. The dog, we say, knows that its master is home. But does it know that Mr. Smith (who is his master), or that the president of the bank (who is that same master), is home? We have no real idea how to settle, or make sense of, these questions. It is much harder to say, when speech is not present, how to distinguish universal thoughts from conjunctions of thoughts, or how to attribute conditional thoughts, or thoughts with, so to speak, mixed quantification ('He hopes that everyone is loved by someone').

These considerations will probably be less persuasive to dog lovers than to others, but in any case they do not constitute an argument. At best what we have shown, or claimed, is that unless there is behaviour that can be interpreted as speech, the evidence will not be adequate to justify the fine distinctions we are used to making in the attribution of thoughts. If we persist in attributing desires, beliefs, or other attitudes under these conditions, our attributions and consequent explanations of actions will be seriously underdetermined in that many alternative systems of attribution, many alternative explanations, will be equally justified by the available data. Perhaps this is all we can say against the attribution of thoughts to dumb creatures; but I do not think so.

Before going on I want to consider a possible objection to the general line I have been pursuing. Suppose we grant, the objector says, that very complex behaviour not observed in infants and elephants is necessary if we are to find application for the full apparatus available for the attribution of thoughts. Still, it may be said, the sketch of how interpretation works does not show that this complexity must be viewed as connected with language. The reason is that the sketch makes too much depend on the special attitude of being thought true. The most direct evidence for the existence of this attitude is honest assertion. But then it would seem that we could treat as speech the behaviour of creatures that never did anything with language except make honest assertions. Some philosophers do dream of such dreary tribes; but would we be right to say they had a language? What has been lost to view is what may be called *the autonomy of meaning*. Once a sentence is understood, an utterance of it may be used to serve almost any extra-linguistic purpose. An instrument that could be put to only one use would lack autonomy of meaning; this amounts to saying it should not be counted as a language. So the complexity of behaviour needed to give full scope to attributions of thought need not, after all, be exactly the same complexity that allows, or requires, interpretation as a language.

I agree with the hypothetical objector that autonomy of meaning is essential to language; indeed it is largely this that explains why linguistic meaning cannot be defined or analysed on the basis of extra-linguistic intentions and beliefs. But the objector fails to distinguish between a language that *could* be used for only one purpose and one that *is* used for only one purpose. An instrument that could be used for only one purpose would not be language. But honest assertion alone might yield a theory of interpretation, and so a language that, though capable of more, might never be put to further uses. (As a practical matter, the event is unthinkable. Someone who knows under what conditions his sentences are socially true cannot fail to grasp, and avail himself of, the possibilities in dishonest assertion—or in joking, story-telling, goading, exaggerating, insulting, and all the rest of the jolly crew.)

A method of interpretation tells us that for speakers of English an utterance of 'It is raining' by a speaker x at time t is true if and only if it is raining (near x) at t. To be armed with this information, and to know that others know it, is to know what an utterance means independently of knowing the purposes that prompted it. The autonomy of meaning also helps to explain how it is possible, by the use of language, to attribute thoughts. Suppose someone utters assertively the sentence 'Snow is white.' Knowing the conditions under which such an utterance is true I can add, if I please, 'I believe that too,' thus attributing a belief to myself. In this case we may both have asserted that snow is white, but sameness of force is not necessary to the self-attribution. The other may say with a sneer, expressing disbelief, 'Snow is white'—and I may again attribute a belief to myself by saying, 'But *I* believe that.' It can work as well in another way: if I can take advantage of an utterance of someone else's to attribute a belief to myself, I can use an utterance of my own to attribute a belief to someone else. First I utter a sentence, perhaps 'Snow is white,' and then I add 'He believes that.' The first utterance may or may not be an assertion; in any case, it does not attribute a belief to anyone (though if it is an assertion, then I do *represent* myself as believing that snow is white). But if my remark 'He believes that' is an assertion, I have attributed a belief to someone else. Finally, there is no bar to my attributing a belief to myself by saying first, 'Snow is white' and then adding, 'I believe that.'

In all these examples, I take the word 'that' to refer demonstratively to an utterance, whether it is an utterance by the speaker of the 'that' or by another speaker. The 'that' cannot refer to a sentence, both because, as Church has pointed out in similar cases, the reference would then have to be relativized to a language, since a sentence may have different meanings in different languages;[1] but also, and more obviously, because the same sentence may have different truth values in the same language.

What demonstrative reference to utterances does in the sort of case just considered it can do as well when the surface structure is altered to something like 'I believe that snow is white' or 'He believes that snow is white.' In these instances also I think we should view the 'that' as a demonstrative, now referring ahead to an utterance on the verge of production. Thus the logical form of standard attributions of attitude is that of two utterances paratactically joined. There is no connective, though the first utterance contains a reference to the second. (Similar remarks go, of course, for inscriptions of sentences.)

I have discussed this analysis of verbal attributions of attitude elsewhere, and there is no need to repeat the arguments and explanations here.[2] It is an analysis with its own difficulties, especially when it comes to analysing quantification into the contained sentence, but I think these difficulties can be overcome while preserving the appealing features of the idea. Here I want to stress a point that connects the paratactic analysis of attribution of attitude with our present theme. The proposed analysis directly relates the autonomous feature of meaning with our ability to describe and attribute thoughts, since it is only because the interpretation of a sentence is independent of its use that the utterance of a sentence can serve in the description of the attitudes of others. If my analysis is right, we can dispense with the unlikely (but common) view that a sentence bracketed into a

[1] Alonzo Church, 'On Carnap's Analysis of Statements of Assertion and Belief', *Analysis*, X (1950), 97–9.
[2] See 'On Saying That', in *Words and Objections: Essays on the Work of W. V. Quine*, eds. D. Davidson and J. Hintikka, Dordrecht, 1969, pp. 158–74.

'that'-clause needs an entirely different interpretation from the one that works for it in other contexts. Since sentences are not names or descriptions in ordinary contexts, we can in particular reject the assumption that the attitudes have objects such as propositions which 'that'-clauses might be held to name or describe. There should be no temptation to call the utterance to which reference is made according to the paratactic analysis the object of the attributed attitude.

Here a facile solution to our problem about the relation between thoughts and speech suggests itself. One way to view the paratactic analysis, a way proposed by Quine in *Word and Object*, is this: when a speaker attributes an attitude to a person, what he does is ape or mimic an actual or possible speech act of that person.[1] Indirect discourse is the best example, and assertion is another good one. Suppose I say, 'Herodotus asserted that the Nile rises in the Mountains of the Moon.' My second utterance—my just past utterance of 'The Nile rises in the Mountains of the Moon'—must, if my attribution to Herodotus is correct, bear a certain relationship to an utterance of Herodotus': it must, in some appropriate sense, be a translation of it. Since, assuming still that the attribution is correct, Herodotus and I are *samesayers*, my utterance mimicked his. Not with respect to force, of course, since I didn't assert anything about the Nile. The sameness is with respect to the content of our utterances. If we turn to other attitudes, the situation is more complicated, for there is typically no utterance to ape. If I affirm 'Jones believes that snow is white,' my utterance of 'Snow is white' may have no actual utterance of Jones's to imitate. Still, we could take the line that what I affirm is that Jones would be honestly speaking his mind were he to utter a sentence translating mine. Given some delicate assumptions about the conditions under which such a subjunctive conditional is true, we could conclude that only someone with a language could have a thought, since to have a thought would be to have a disposition to utter certain sentences with appropriate force under given circumstances.

We could take this line, but unfortunately there seems no clear reason why we have to. We set out to find an argument to show that only creatures with speech have thoughts. What has just been outlined is not an argument, but a proposal, and a proposal we need not accept. The paratactic analysis of the logical form of attributions of

---

[1] W. V. Quine, *Word and Object*, Cambridge, Mass., 1960, p. 219.

attitude can get along without the mimic-theory of utterance. When I say, 'Jones believes that snow is white' I describe Jones's state of mind directly: it is indeed the state of mind someone is in who could honestly assert 'Snow is white' if he spoke English, but that may be a state a languageless creature could also be in.

In order to make my final main point, I must return to an aspect of interpretation so far neglected. I remarked that the attitude of holding true, directed to sentences under specified circumstances, is the basis for interpretation, but I did not say how it can serve this function. The difficulty, it will be remembered, is that a sentence is held true because of two factors: what the holder takes the sentence to mean, and what he believes. In order to sort things out, what is needed is a method for holding one factor steady while the other is studied.

Membership in a language community depends on the ability to interpret the utterances of members of the group, and a method is at hand if one has, and knows one has, a theory which provides truth conditions, more or less in Tarski's style, for all sentences (relativized, as always, to time and speaker). The theory is correct as long as it entails, by finitely stated means, theorems of the familiar form: ' "It is raining" is true for a speaker x at time t if and only if it is raining (near x) at t.' The evidential basis for such a theory concerns sentences held true, facts like the following: ' "It is raining" is held true by Smith at 8 a.m. on 26 August and it did rain near Smith at that time.' It would be possible to generate a correct theory simply by considering sentences to be true when held true, provided (1) there was a theory which satisfied the formal constraints and was consistent in this way with the evidence, and (2) all speakers held a sentence to be true just when that sentence was true—provided, that is, all beliefs, at least as far as they could be expressed, were correct.

But of course it cannot be assumed that speakers never have false beliefs. Error is what gives belief its point. We can, however, take it as given that *most* beliefs are correct. The reason for this is that a belief is identified by its location in a pattern of beliefs; it is this pattern that determines the subject matter of the belief, what the belief is about. Before some object in, or aspect of, the world can become part of the subject matter of a belief (true or false) there must be endless true beliefs about the subject matter. False beliefs tend to undermine the identification of the subject matter; to undermine, therefore, the validity of a description of the belief as being about that subject. And so, in turn, false beliefs undermine the claim that a connected belief is false. To take an example, how clear are we that the ancients—some ancients—believed that the earth was flat? *This* earth? Well, this earth of ours is part of the solar system, a system partly identified by the fact that it is a gaggle of large, cool, solid bodies circling around a very large, hot star. If someone believes *none* of this about the earth, is it certain that it is the earth that he is thinking about? An answer is not called for. The point is made if this kind of consideration of related beliefs can shake one's confidence that the ancients believed the earth was flat. It isn't that any one false belief necessarily destroys our ability to identify further beliefs, but that the intelligibility of such identifications must depend on a background of largely unmentioned and unquestioned true beliefs. To put it another way: the more things a believer is right about, the sharper his errors are. Too much mistake simply blurs the focus.

What makes interpretation possible, then, is the fact that we can dismiss *a priori* the chance of massive error. A theory of interpretation cannot be correct that makes a man assent to very many false sentences: it must generally be the case that a sentence is true when a speaker holds it to be. So far as it goes, it is in favour of a method of interpretation that it counts a sentence true just when speakers hold it to be true. But of course, the speaker may be wrong; and so may the interpreter. So in the end what must be counted in favour of a method of interpretation is that it puts the interpreter in general agreement with the speaker: according to the method, the speaker holds a sentence true under specified conditions, and these conditions obtain, in the opinion of the interpreter, just when the speaker holds the sentence to be true.

No simple theory can put a speaker and interpreter in perfect agreement, and so a workable theory must from time to time assume error on the part of one or the other. The basic methodological precept is, therefore, that a good theory of interpretation maximizes agreement. Or, given that sentences are infinite in number, and given further considerations to come, a better word might be *optimize*.

Some disagreements are more destructive of understanding than others, and a sophisticated theory must naturally take this into account. Disagreement about theoretical matters may (in some cases) be more tolerable than disagreement about what is more evident; disagreement about how things look or appear is less tolerable than disagreement about how they are; disagreement about the truth of attributions of certain attitudes to a speaker by that same speaker may not be tolerable at all, or barely. It is impossible to simplify the considerations that are relevant, for everything we know or believe about the way evidence supports belief can be put to work in deciding where the theory can best allow error, and what errors are least destructive of understanding. The methodology of interpretation is, in this respect, nothing but epistemology seen in the mirror of meaning.

The interpreter who assumes his method can be made to work for a language community will strive for a theory that optimizes agreement throughout the community. Since easy communication has survival value, he may expect usage within a community to favour simple common theories of interpretation.

If this account of radical interpretation is right, at least in broad outline, then we should acknowledge that the concepts of objective truth, and of error, necessarily emerge in the context of interpretation. The distinction between a sentence being held true and being in fact true is essential to the existence of an interpersonal system of communication, and when in individual cases there is a difference, it must be counted as error. Since the attitude of holding true is the same, whether the sentence is true or not, it corresponds directly to belief. The concept of belief thus stands ready to take up the slack between objective truth and the held true, and we come to understand it just in this connection.

We have the idea of belief only from the role of belief in the interpretation of language, for as a private attitude it is not intelligible except as an adjustment to the public norm provided by language. It follows that a creature must be a member of a speech community if it is to have the concept of belief. And given the dependence of other attitudes on belief, we can say more generally that only a creature that can interpret speech can have the concept of a thought.

Can a creature have a belief if it does not have the concept of belief? It seems to me it cannot, and for this reason. Someone cannot have a belief unless he understands the possibility of being mistaken, and this requires grasping the contrast between truth and error—true belief and false belief. But this contrast, I have argued, can emerge only in the context of interpretation, which alone forces us to the idea of an objective, public truth.

It is often wrongly thought that the semantical concept of truth is redundant, that there is no difference between asserting that a sentence s is true, and using s to make an assertion. What may be right is a redundancy theory of belief, that to believe that *p* is not to be distinguished from the belief that *p* is true. This notion of truth is not the semantical notion: language is not directly in the picture. But it is only just out of the picture; it is part of the frame. For the notion of a true belief depends on the notion of a true utterance, and this in turn there cannot be without shared language. As Ulysses was made to put it by a member of our speech community:

> . . . no man is the lord of anything,
> Though in and of him there be much consisting,
> Till he communicate his parts to others;
> Nor doth he of himself know them for aught
> Till he behold them formed in th'applause
> Where they're extended.

> (*Troilus and Cressida*, III. iii. 115–20.)

2 Meaning and Experience

D. FØLLESDAL

MEANING is a central concern in contemporary philosophy; not just in the so-called analytic varieties, but in the non-analytic ones as well. However, while in non-analytic philosophy a recurrent theme and a main reason for the interest in meaning has been a conviction that meaning and experience are intimately tied together, that experience is permeated with meaning, analytic philosophers have been more concerned with linguistic meaning, meaning as expressed in language. Analytic philosophers have also shown a growing interest in the connection between meaning and various kinds of intensional phenomena such as belief, other propositional attitudes, and perception. However, the more prominent meaning becomes, the more important it is to get clear about how we can know anything about meaning. As a consequence, a main question in recent analytic philosophy has been in what way experience serves as *evidence* for our judgements concerning meaning. This latter question was very important for Professor Davidson's arguments concerning thought and talk in the first essay in this series,[1] and it will be my main subject. But before I turn to it, I want to say something about various non-analytic philosophers' views on meaning and experience, and particularly something about how meaning is said to permeate our experience, since this will be important for what I shall afterwards say about experience as evidence for judgements concerning meaning.

The 'school' in contemporary non-analytic philosophy which most explicitly and carefully has focused on how experience is connected with meaning is phenomenology. The main concern of phenomenology is to study that which distinguishes man from the physical world, and this, phenomenologists maintain, is mind or consciousness.

[1] See above, pp. 7–23.

According to Edmund Husserl, the founder of phenomenology, what characterize consciousness are certain features that make consciousness always seem to be consciousness *of* something. Husserl held that whenever we see or think, there seems to be an object which we see or of which we think, and similarly for other acts of consciousness. These features of an act, in virtue of which it seems to have an object, Husserl calls the *noema* of the act, from greek νόημα, that which is grasped in thought.

The relation between the noema and the object of an act is like the relation between the meaning and reference of a linguistic expression. The object of an act is a function of the act's noema if the act has an object; some acts turn out not to have any, although, like the definite singular terms in our language, they always appear to have an object. Conversely, however, a noema is not a function of the object since to one object there may correspond several different noemata, depending on the different ways in which the object can be experienced, whether one perceives it, imagines it, remembers it, etc., and depending also on its orientation, one's point of view, etc. The noema is that manifold of determinations which unifies the different components of consciousness in such a way that we have an experience as of one full-fledged object. Thus, when, for example, we see a tree, we see something which has a back and many other features that we cannot see from where we are. We do not see the back, but we see something that has a back, and we expect to find this and various other features when we go on exploring the tree using our various senses. The senses do not provide data from which we infer that there are physical objects, nor do they provide data that are organized into physical objects. They do not provide data at all. We do not see what is going on at our sense organs, we see physical objects. The irritations of our sensory surfaces do not supply data, but provide only boundary conditions that the noema in our act has to satisfy. The irritations of our sensory surfaces never suffice to uniquely determine what the noema of the act is going to be, but only cut down on the variety of noemata we can have in the given situation. Wittgenstein's duck–rabbit example can be used to illustrate this, though it is not quite a parallel, since in the duck–rabbit case there is a physical object, viz. the figure on paper, that is alternately seen as a duck and rabbit, while in the case of perception there is no physical object that plays a role similar to the figure on the paper; there are, according to Husserl, no data or other objects that are 'taken' in different ways.

Husserl, who regarded the noema as 'a generalization of the notion of meaning to the realm of all acts',[1] was well aware of the question of how we come to know anything about noemata. He held that statements about noemata could not be reduced to statements about physical phenomena, and that the methods of natural science could not clarify this realm of meaning. Still we can explore it, he said, by the phenomenological method. This method consists in a special reflection, which Husserl calls the transcendental reduction, in which we make the noema in one act an object of a different act, an act of reflection.

Husserl went to great lengths to explain and apply his method, but many of his students and close collaborators, including Heidegger, whom Husserl regarded as one of the best, held that the transcendental reduction is impossible. We shall come briefly back to this later, but Husserl was in any case fully aware that some special method was needed in order that his theory of 'meaning and experience' should become more than just an elaborate terminology.

The foremost proponents of contemporary existentialism, Heidegger and Sartre, both started out from Husserl. There is an isomorphism between their philosophies and Husserl's phenomenology. Husserl remarks in several places in the margin of his copy of Heidegger's *Sein und Zeit*: 'What Heidegger says here is just what I say there and there, but translated into a deep-sounding terminology.' (Sometimes Husserl adds 'and robbed of every justification'.) What is new and interesting in Heidegger is mainly that he regards meaning as being found in and brought about by *all kinds* of human activity, and does not treat it as something belonging purely in the *theoretical* sphere, as had been common in theories of meaning. There are some similar ideas in Husserl's unpublished manuscripts from 1918 on. However, Heidegger, in 1927, some years before the later Wittgenstein, made it a major theme. In Sartre there are similar ideas, but Sartre focuses on other points; mainly on how all human activity, because it is inseparable from meaning, is free in spite of the apparent determinacy of the physical. This is a theme that Donald Davidson has developed further, with more precision, more argument, and no doubt quite independently in 'Mental Events'[2] and other works.

[1] Edmund Husserl, *Ideen*, Vol. III (*Husserliana*, Vol. V), The Hague: Nijhoff, 1952, p. 89.
[2] Donald Davidson, 'Mental Events', in *Experience and Theory*, ed. Lawrence Foster and J. W. Swanson, Amherst: Univ. of Massachusetts Press, 1970.

28   *D. Føllesdal*

The other main trends in contemporary non-analytic philosophy also have meaning as their central theme: the neo-hermeneuticists, Gadamer and others, hold, inspired by Husserl and Heidegger, that all grasping of meaning, in understanding and interpretation, presupposes extensive agreement concerning what is true and what is false, and they explore the consequences of this. Meaning also plays a central role in structuralism and even in the writings of some neo-Marxists. However, we shall not consider these schools here, but turn to analytic philosophy, and the problem of experience as *evidence* for our judgements concerning meaning.

The question concerning experience as evidence for our judgements concerning meaning has become more and more prominent in analytic philosophy over the past twenty years, largely due to the work of Professor Quine, who first asked it in 'Two Dogmas of Empiricism'[1] in 1950, and has pursued it further in *Word and Object*[2] and several other books and articles.

In this lecture I shall not give any detailed exposition of Quine's views. I shall limit myself to emphasizing, as I go along, some points that Quine and others have made that are important for my discussion, and that tend to be overlooked or misunderstood.

The starting-point is empiricism: roughly the view that all our evidence reaches us through our senses. I fully accept this, although it is what gives rise to all the difficulties concerning meaning that we are now going into.

The empiricist view on evidence can be made more precise in various mutually incompatible ways. However, all that we need for our immediate purposes is the following feature that all varieties of empiricism seem to share: the evidence available to us, even if it were all in, leaves our choice of a theory of nature under-determined.[3] Several mutually incompatible theories of nature would be compatible with the evidence. This under-determination does not mean that these theories are all equally good. Some of them are more acceptable than others, because of their simplicity and other factors. We have reason to believe that the sentences of such well-confirmed theories are true and that the entities assumed by them exist.

[1] W. V. Quine, 'Two Dogmas of Empiricism', in *From a Logical Point of View*, Cambridge, Mass.: Harvard Univ. Press, 1953; 2nd edn., 1961.
[2] W. V. Quine, *Word and Object*, Cambridge, Mass.: M.I.T. Press, 1960.
[3] By 'theory' is here meant a structure of sentences which are interconnected with one another in such a way that they share their evidential support. For more details on this topic, see Quine, *Word and Object*, pp. 11 ff.

One's theory of nature should exhaust all the evidence one has, and now I will stress a point which will be important for my argument: the entities that one should assume there to be, are those and only those that are assumed by one's theory of nature, that is, those that seem needed to account for all the evidence in as simple and otherwise satisfactory a manner as possible. These entities may include physical objects and classes, but also various other entities, if such would help us to account for the evidence. The problem with theories about intensional entities is that they do not serve any such useful purpose, but belong in eddies that, as Quine has argued in 'Two Dogmas of Empiricism', are completely separated from those parts of our theory of nature which help account for our experience.

Given this much about theories of nature, consider the notion of meaning. Even after all the evidence has been accounted for, there remains the problem of communicating one's insights to others, that is, correlating two theories. Obviously, not every correlation will do. One condition that traditionally has been imposed on such correlation, or translation, is that expressions shall be correlated with one another if they express the same meaning. Now, as long as intensional entities are not called for within the theory of nature in order to account for the evidence, there is no reason to believe that there are such entities, nor do we have identity criteria for them. We noted earlier that Husserl thought that we could explore such entities through 'transcendental reduction'. However, we also noted that the reduction was problematic. Moreover, Husserl said nothing about the identity criteria for these intensional entities. The condition that expressions correlated with one another must express the same meaning is no condition at all. It does not eliminate any possible correlation, since it does not provide for any evidence to count against any possible correlation. Far less, of course, would such a condition impose uniqueness of translation. It is one of Quine's many contributions to philosophy to have pointed out, in 'Two Dogmas of Empiricism', the emptiness of such traditional theories of meaning.

What we are after is a way of separating out, in every sentence of our theory, one component, its meaning, which can then be correlated with corresponding meaning-components in another's theory. Quine claims in 'Two Dogmas' and, with more detail and argument, in *Word and Object*, that there is no distinction to be drawn, generally, between meaning and information. They are inseparably intertwined, and this inseparability of meaning and information is the crux of what Quine calls 'indeterminacy of translation'.

In order to get to this conclusion, Quine makes, however, one crucial assumption about meaning. 'Suppose,' he says, 'we hold with the old empiricist Peirce, that the very meaning of a statement consists in the difference its truth would make to possible experience.'[1] Quine then argues that from this 'verification theory of meaning', together with the under-determination of a theory of nature, indeterminacy of translation follows. That is, two languages may be translated into one another in numerous ways, all of which are equally compatible with all the evidence. And further, there is no reason to regard any of these translations as more correct than any of the others. Or, as Quine also puts it, 'the empirical meanings of typical statements about the external world are inaccessible and ineffable'.[2]

The gist of Quine's argument is that given the under-determination of our theory of nature, some sentences, at least, in our theory are not tied up with any particular pieces of evidence, or experience, but relate via the whole intervening theory to all of them. Thus such a sentence, to quote Quine, 'has no fund of experiential implications it can call its own'.[3] Quine's point is not just an *epistemological* one, that we are not able to separate meaning from information, but the *metaphysical* one, that there are not two such items to be separated— given, of course, that meaning is what Peirce said it is. This is the point of *in*determinacy as opposed to the *under*-determination of natural science, where there is something to be right or wrong about.

The observation that individual sentences are not tested against experience one by one, but only via the theory as a whole, was, as Quine notes, a main point in Pierre Duhem's philosophy of science. We can therefore summarize Quine's argument in the following formula:

Duhem plus *Peirce* yields *Indeterminacy*.

Quine is fully aware that the verification theory of meaning is an assumption on his part, and he asks in 'Epistemology Naturalized': 'Should the unwelcomeness of the conclusion persuade us to abandon the verification theory of meaning?'[4] 'Certainly not,' Quine answers,

---

[1] 'Epistemology Naturalized', *Ontological Relativity and Other Essays*, New York: Columbia Univ. Press, 1969, p. 78.
[2] Ibid., pp. 78–9.
[3] Ibid., pp. 79 and 82.
[4] 'Epistemology Naturalized', p. 81.

and the reason he gives for this is important, for it shows that Quine's basic reason for assuming the verification theory of meaning is that he takes it for granted that there is no other kind of empirical meaning. I quote the passage in full, italicizing what I take to be important:

Should the unwelcomeness of the conclusion persuade us to abandon the verification theory of meaning? Certainly not. *The sort of meaning that is basic for translation, and to the learning of one's own language, is necessarily empirical meaning and nothing more. Surely one has no choice but to be an empiricist so far as one's theory of linguistic meaning is concerned.*[1]

One may agree with Quine that we need an empirical theory of meaning, and still not agree that we need a verification theory of meaning. For the latter conclusion follows from the former only if the verification theory of meaning is the only empirical theory—something we need not take for granted. We must distinguish, I think, between two notions: empirical meaning and an empirical *theory* of meaning. We may then perhaps grant that the label 'empirical meaning' can be reserved for the notion of meaning that the verificationists, such as Peirce and the logical empiricists, were after. That is, a notion where the meaning of a sentence is equated with the difference its truth would make to possible experience. But we have to distinguish this from an empirical *theory* of meaning, that is a theory of meaning according to which our judgements concerning meaning are based on evidence that reaches us through our senses. It is this latter notion we have in mind when we hold that our theory of meaning must be empirical. The verification theory of meaning may be empirical in this sense, too, but as we shall see, there are alternative theories of meaning that are none the less empirical.

Hence, although it is part of our empiricism that communication and language learning must rest ultimately on sensory evidence, all we may conclude from this is that our theory of meaning must be *empirical*, not that it must be the *verification* theory of meaning.

Clearly, not all empirical theories of meaning are adequate. What, then, is this notion of meaning that we are out to capture? Part of my aim in this lecture is to bring out a little more clearly what we are after when we discuss meaning.

Before we leave the issue of empirical meaning v. an empirical theory of meaning we should note that the decision whether or not to keep the verification theory of meaning is no minor decision. As we

[1] 'Epistemology Naturalized', p. 81.

have seen, the verification theory of meaning is one of the basic premisses in Quine's argument for indeterminacy of translation. If, therefore, the verification theory has to be replaced by some other theory of meaning, the whole issue of indeterminacy has to be rethought anew, although, as we shall now see, indeterminacy of translation is likely to carry over to other empirical theories of meaning as well.

The reason for this is the following: A translation, as we have noted, can be regarded as a special kind of correlation of expressions in one language with expressions in another (possibly the same language). Different theories of meaning impose different conditions on those correlations. The classical theory of meaning that we find in Frege, Husserl, and many others requires that expressions should be correlated only if they express the same meaning. This condition appears to guarantee uniqueness of translation until one observes, as Quine did, that it is empty. Other conditions, for example those that Quine imposes on translation in *Word and Object*, do not guarantee uniqueness, but leave room for many different correlations. This is what Quine calls indeterminacy of translation.

Critics of Quine, such as Chomsky,[1] Rorty,[2] and many others, have argued that this just makes translation like empirical theory. There, too, we have certain boundary conditions that have to be satisfied. A number of mutually incompatible theories satisfy them, but on the basis of simplicity, etc. we settle for one of them and regard it as true. Why not do the same in translation? The answer is, I think, and this is a point that nobody who has discussed Quine's views appears to have fully understood: all the truths there are, are included in our theory of nature. As we noted earlier, in our theory of nature we try to account for *all* our experiences. And the only entities we are justified in assuming are those that are appealed to in the simplest theory that accounts for all this evidence. These entities and their properties and interrelations are all there is to the world, and all there is to be right or wrong about. All truths about these are included in our theory of nature. In translation we are not describing a further realm of reality, we are just correlating two comprehensive theories concerning all there is. In doing this, we use some of the same evidence

[1] Noam Chomsky, 'Quine's Empirical Assumptions', in *Words and Objections: Essays on the Work of W. V. Quine*, ed. Donald Davidson and Jaakko Hintikka, Dordrecht: Reidel, 1969, pp. 53–68.
[2] Richard Rorty, 'Indeterminacy of Translation and of Truth', *Synthese* XXIII (1972), 443–62.

over again, but for a different purpose. Our aim is not to describe the world, but to correlate two such descriptions. This is, I think, the reason for the difference between theory of nature and translation, and thereby for indeterminacy of translation. It is not stated in this way in any of Quine's writings, but it seems to fit in well with what Quine says on this topic. When Quine says that in translation there is generally nothing to be right or wrong about, he is, it seems, not just stating an ontological dogma to the effect that there are no propositions or other intensional entities; although he sometimes says that he is only expressing a bias towards physicalism. It seems to me that Quine's position is more interesting if his ontological bias towards physicalism is regarded as a consequence of a more fundamental epistemological bias towards empiricism.

As you will have noted, in this second argument for indeterminacy, nothing at all was said about the particular conditions that Quine puts on translation. Hence this argument applies to all theories of meaning, and it seems that we have established the following thesis:

Any theory of meaning, whether verificational or not, that does not yield a unique scheme of translation, leads to indeterminacy of translation, and not to just the under-determination characteristic of physical theory.

This is not a 'deep' thesis, it is just another way of expressing the difference between translation and empirical theory that we just discussed. However, with this thesis in hand, we can usually see very quickly whether a theory of meaning leads to indeterminacy of translation.

What, then, are the conditions we should put on a correlation between two languages in order to regard it as a translation? We shall now compare the virtues and drawbacks of two such sets of conditions that have been proposed by Quine and Davidson, respectively, in order to see more clearly what notion of meaning we are after.

Quine, as we could expect in view of his verification theory of meaning, assigns great importance to what is occurring at our sensory surfaces and how this is correlated with our linguistic behaviour. In order to describe what is going on at a person's sensory surfaces without begging questions of meaning, Quine introduces a notion of stimulation in terms of which he formulates various conditions on translation. These conditions turn on equating the stimulations that are had by different subjects. In Quine's theory of language, equating of stimulations of different subjects is the basis for all communication, and communication is just what language is for, as has often been argued.

However, as Quine himself has pointed out, the notion of equating one person's stimulation with another's, which is basic for his whole theory of meaning, is highly problematic. We shall now consider this problem. This will, I think, teach us something about experience and meaning.

Quine discusses the problem in the last pages of his book *Ontological Relativity*. While in *Word and Object* a stimulation is said to be the evolving pattern of, for example, chromatic irradiation of the eye,[1] Quine says in *Ontological Relativity* that he sees no fault in defining the sensory stimulation of a person as the triggering of all of a sub-class of his sensory receptors.[2] Now, while this may work well for comparisons between stimulations affecting one and the same person, it leads immediately to problems when we come to intersubjective comparisons. Quine says: 'When it comes to the intersubjective, however, perhaps the most we can realistically speak of is resemblance and not identity of stimulation patterns. All stimulation patterns should perhaps be viewed as peculiar to individual subjects, and as bearing intersubjective resemblances, at best, based on approximate homologies of nerve endings.'[3]

Quine suggests that for members of the same species there is, perhaps, enough homology of nerve endings to enable us to speak of resemblance of stimulation patterns, while no such homology might be found, for example, between Martians and humans. Quine therefore ends the book with the open problem of 'saying in general what it means for two subjects to get the same stimulation or, failing that, what it means for two subjects to get more nearly the same stimulation than two others'.

In criticism of this proposal of Quine's, I would like to suggest that identifying stimulations with triggering of nerve endings sets us off on a wrong track. By talking about the triggering of the sensory receptors we are already going too deeply inside the skin. Language being a social phenomenon, the basis for language learning and communication should also be publicly accessible without the aid of neurophysiology. This is a point repeatedly emphasized by Quine himself. In

---

[1] W. V. Quine, *Word and Object*, p. 31.
[2] W. V. Quine, *Ontological Relativity*, p. 158
[3] Ibid., p. 159.

fact, on page 157 of *Ontological Relativity* he says that homology of receptors 'ought not to matter'. What, then, would be an alternative way of describing the evidence that we get through our senses and upon which communication and language learning is based?

One alternative would be to identify stimulations not with the pattern of triggered nerve endings, but, as suggested by the terminology in *Word and Object*, with the pattern of chromatic irradiation, sound vibration, etc., just outside, or *at* the sensory surfaces. What goes on inside the surfaces, in nerve endings, nerves, and the brain, is not part of the evidence upon which communication and language learning is based, but is a product of the individual's adjustments to his surroundings and his language community. This alternative approach must, to avoid various difficulties, be based upon a theory of what parts of a person's surface are sensitive to what kind of stimulation. This would be a matter of empirical study, for example in behavioural psychology and neural physiology. In our ordinary communication with other humans we have, by second nature, long made use of such a theory based on similarities between human bodies.

A visual stimulation would then be very like a photograph taken at the eye, with the camera oriented in the same direction as the eye. A main advantage of this notion of stimulation is that the stimulations would be readily comparable from one subject to another. Due to differences of peripheral vision, etc., the relevant stimulations would not usually be identical from person to person, but nevertheless there would be a good deal of overlap. What is important, is that for every such difficulty in connection with *this* notion of stimulation there seems to be a corresponding and usually more serious difficulty in connection with the old notion. So, in balance, this new notion, which has important advantages and does not appear to give rise to any new difficulties, seems to me to be definitely preferable to the old.

Of course, as Quine has pointed out,[1] what we usually do is assume that people get the same stimulations when they are in the same position and same orientation towards the same physical bodies and forces. It is only where this view leads to difficulties, for example because people have different shapes and sizes, that we need to fall back on the more technical notion of stimulation.

However, there is another, more fundamental, problem that arises regardless of how we try to define or explicate stimulation and regardless of all adjustments we make to overcome the various difficulties I

[1] *Ontological Relativity*, p. 159.

have mentioned. This is the problem that meaning permeates all our experience. We have already observed, in connection with Husserl, that although everything remains the same in our physical surroundings and on our sensory surface, what I experience, what I see, may vary greatly. As we noted, we may see a duck or a rabbit, depending on, as Husserl would have put it, our noema. Of course, the duck–rabbit example is an extreme one, involving as it does the flipping back and forth between two ways of organizing experience. But what goes on at our sensory surfaces *never* uniquely determines what object it is that we experience. We become especially aware of this after instances of misperception, when suddenly what we see is very different from what we saw before. This was one of Husserl's main points, and I think he was right.

Among the consequences of this for the notion of stimulus meaning I shall mention only one: In trying to determine under what conditions a person assents to or dissents from, for example, the one-word sentence 'Rabbit', we risk that the person in the same stimulus situation fluctuates back and forth between assenting to and dissenting from the sentence 'Rabbit', depending on whether he takes what he sees as a rabbit or, for example, as a duck. Similarly, for any other sentence a person may change from assenting to dissenting although the stimulus situation remains the same. These variations in the dispositions to assent and dissent, from time to time and from person to person, might seem to eliminate almost completely the class of observation sentences, which are so crucial to Quine's theory of meaning and translation. It might seem that not even 'Rabbit', Quine's pet example, comes out an observation sentence. However, there is one feature of Quine's theory that counteracts this: in investigating stimulus meanings, one is always querying the subject before one gets his response. Thus, for example, one asks in a given stimulus situation: 'Rabbit?' and then awaits the response. This query may be enough to bring the subject to see what he has in front of him as a rabbit. So the querying procedure tends to produce more stability in people's responses than one would otherwise expect.

The theory of stimulations and stimulus meaning is, as we have seen, full of difficulties. No wonder, then, that philosophers have tried to develop alternatives to Quine's theory of meaning; alternatives which do not make use of such problematic notions. One such alternative, which it would be instructive to contrast with Quine's, is Davidson's. I shall now turn to this theory of meaning.

Davidson's theory is usually so closely associated with Quine's that people fail to see the differences between them. This is largely due to the fact that Davidson's basic point, that in translation one should try to maximize agreement, is also found in Quine. However, this point has importantly different status in the two theories. I shall now sketch Davidson's theory of meaning, and emphasize how it differs from Quine's. As we shall see, we here have a theory of meaning which is empirical, but not verificational.

Davidson focuses on meaning for one language rather than on translation between languages. For comparison with Quine, however, I will consider Davidson's theory of translation. He imposes two conditions on translation. First, the translation must carry over from one language to the other all the structure that is needed for a theory of truth; and this is a considerable amount of structure. Davidson and Wallace have argued that it includes, for example, the distinction between singular and general terms, which Quine regards as subject to indeterminacy. Be this as it may, this first condition on translation does not make our notion of translation non-empirical. Secondly, Davidson requires translation to be such as to maximize agreement; that is, in translating A's language into B's, sentences that A assents to should as much as possible translate into sentences that B assents to and conversely; correspondingly for dissent. This requirement, too, seems to be as empirical as the requirements Quine puts on translation. Quine, also, assumes that we can recognize assent and dissent in the native's behaviour, and Davidson requires no further assumptions.

Now, Quine too, in *Word and Object*[1] and elsewhere, formulates as a maxim of translation that assertions which seem at face value strikingly false should be regarded as indicative of differences of language and not of belief. Quine regards this principle as so fundamental to translation that he even includes as one of his conditions on translation that truth functions shall be preserved. For, to quote Quine, 'The more absurd or exotic the beliefs imputed to a people, the more suspicious we are entitled to be of the translations: the myth of the prelogical people marks only the extreme. For translation theory, banal messages are the breath of life.'[2] It seems to me that here we

---

[1] *Word and Object*, pp. 59 and 69. Compare also Neil Wilson's 'principle of charity', in 'Substances without Substrata', *Review of Metaphysics* XII (1959), 521–39.

[2] *Word and Object*, p. 69.

38   D. Føllesdal

have a different strain in Quine's theory of meaning, unrelated to the verificationist idea that underlies his other conditions on translation.

The crucial difference between Davidson and Quine is that while for Davidson maximizing agreement is the main basis for translation, it is for Quine just one among several such bases; the others all concern stimulus meaning. *The notion of stimulation, or sensory experience, which is the main basis of meaning for Quine, plays no role whatsoever in Davidson's theory.*

Clearly, Davidson's theory leaves us with indeterminacy of translation. For although the conditions Davidson puts on translation cut down considerably the number of correlations between languages that qualify as translations, they clearly do not leave us with a unique correlation. And therefore, according to the thesis we formulated earlier, we have indeterminacy of translation.

We have now considered two theories of meaning which clearly can be called empirical. It is immediately obvious that numerous others can be constructed by imposing various restrictions on the correlations that qualify as translations; the basic evidence being all the time restricted to what reaches us through our senses. Which restrictions, however, correspond most closely to the notion of meaning we are after? This question is best answered, I think, by considering various candidates for such restrictions and studying their consequences. In this way we can either reject them out of hand, or see how they must be modified or supplemented by further restrictions.

Let us start with Davidson's requirement that translation must preserve enough structure for a theory of truth. It seems to me that this is an important insight. As Davidson has pointed out, there are several good reasons for this requirement; for example, it seems to be needed for language learning. As Davidson puts it in 'Truth and Meaning': any satisfactory theory of meaning must give an account of how the truth conditions of each sentence relate 'to those aspects ("words") of the sentence that *recur* in other sentences, and can be assigned identical roles in other sentences'.[1] Consequently, it seems that this idea of Davidson's clearly belongs in any satisfactory theory of meaning.

Davidson's second condition, that agreement should be maximized, also stresses what seems to be an important factor in meaning and communication. At the beginning of this paper, in discussing non-

[1] Donald Davidson, 'Truth and Meaning', *Synthese* XVII (1967), 311.

analytic philosophy, we noted that Gadamer and other hermeneuti-
cists hold that all understanding and interpretation presupposes
extensive agreement concerning what is true and what is false. Similar
observations have been made by Wittgenstein and many other philosophers. I have quoted several passages where Quine argues for his
more limited version of the condition, namely that one should preserve agreement with regard to what one considers obvious.

In his essay in this series Davidson supports this condition with
several further arguments, and more arguments could be added. Thus,
for example, let us consider the purposes of language and communication. One important such purpose seems to be to achieve agreement.
When one asserts a sentence, it is often in order to get others to
believe something. Questions often aim at getting information, that is,
coming to know and possibly share the beliefs of others; similarly for
other uses of language. We know from experience that it is usually
easier to bring somebody into agreement with us if we agree on a good
deal at the outset. So a pragmatist could perhaps give the following
justification for maximizing agreement in translations: maximize
agreement in order to maximize agreement.

However, although a certain amount of agreement is clearly important for communication and meaning, it cannot be so exclusively
important as it is in Davidson's theory of meaning. I shall now argue
that the condition 'Maximize agreement' has to be tempered with
other conditions that concern what is going on at our sensory
surfaces, and that it is a definite weakness of Davidson's theory that
the notion of sensory experience plays no role in it.

It seems obvious to me that agreement on highly observational
sentences in appropriate observational situations is much more
important than agreement on more theoretical sentences, and that
consideration of the irritations of our sensory surfaces is particularly
crucial. Thus, for example, if a native dissents from a sentence that I
am inclined to translate as 'Rabbit here', while I assent to the latter
sentence, I will no longer give any weight to our disagreement if I
discover that the rabbit that I see is hidden to the native by a big tree.
Hence, it seems that in maximizing agreement, one cannot simply
count sentences, but must weight sentences in accordance, among
other things, with the evidence relations that obtain between them.
Last year, I discussed this with Davidson, who informed me that he
intends his theory to be based on weighted agreement, so that, for
example, in building up a theory of meaning for a language, if a

speaker holds true a statement of the type 'it seems to me that' it is very important that the theory of meaning accords truth to it. I consider such a theory of weighted agreement to be a most promising approach to meaning and translation. Through it, one can take into account the way in which a person reasons and tries to justify his beliefs. In doing this, one assumes, of course, that the other person is, at least to some extent, rational, like oneself. Such an assumption of rationality seems, however, to be basic to understanding and communication. In fact, I regard it as even more basic than agreement. It is, I believe, our main reason for emphasizing agreement, especially with regard to what we consider obvious.

Still, such a theory of weighted agreement does not relieve the translator and student of meaning from considering what is happening at our sensory surfaces. On the contrary, a main source of evidence for a rational person is his sensory experience. For this reason, a special premium must be put on agreement between similarly placed observers. And this notion of similarly placed observers brings us directly back to the problem of intersubjective comparisons of stimulations that we discussed in connection with Quine. Hence, *in a satisfactory theory of meaning there seems to be no way of avoiding the study of sensory experience.*

We have now discussed some conditions on translation, and we have argued that a theory of meaning should include at least the following:

(1) Davidson's condition concerning the structure needed for a theory of truth.
(2) A condition concerning weighted agreement, in which what is going on at our sensory surfaces plays an important role.

However, there is clearly more evidence that has to be taken into account and that will lead to further conditions. I shall end my paper by pointing to *three* such types of evidence:

First, in all the work that has been done on evidence concerning judgements of meaning, attention has been limited to sentences and assent and dissent. Quine even explicitly confines the evidential basis to observation of assent and dissent elicited by querying certain sentences in various stimulus situations. He says: 'Any realistic theory of evidence must be inseparable from the psychology of stimulus and response, applied to sentences.'[1]

---

[1] *Word and Object*, p. 17.

It seems obvious to me, however, that we have to take into account much more evidence than this, even if we insist on remaining empiricists. The kind of behaviourism that an empiricist seems committed to is much broader than a psychology of stimulus and response. In studying man, and meaning, we have to observe and take into account all the sensory evidence that is available. Thus, we have to observe not only verbal behaviour in stimulus–response situations, but also spontaneous verbal behaviour, which does not seem to be triggered by any observable stimulation.

Further, we must not limit ourselves to studying the use of language in assertion and expression of assent and dissent. We must consider other uses of language, such as questions, commands, promises, etc.

Secondly, other language-related activities, like ostension, must be taken into account. Thus, for example, ostension seems to give us valuable clues to what a person is referring to, which, so far, have been neglected in the literature on evidence for judgements concerning meaning.

Now, as Quine has argued in several places, particularly in *Ontological Relativity*, reference is behaviourally inscrutable.[1] This means that no amount of pointing to objects, or observing other people doing so, together with observations of these people's verbal behaviour, can uniquely determine how the locutions of others should be correlated with ours. However, such observations still serve to show that some translational schemes are inadequate, and hence provide evidence that should be taken into account by our theory of meaning.

As long as the evidence remains restricted to assent to or dissent from sentences, then—whether one requires translation to maximize agreement generally (Davidson) or only with respect to some select sentences under certain stimulus conditions (Quine)—the objects a person is taken as referring to are, presumably, any entities which make these sentences come out true, according to our lights. However, as soon as we broaden our base and include in our evidence observation of ostension, the situation becomes different. By observing what a person points to, we may often come to see that the person refers to an object that, according to our lights, does not satisfy the sentences he asserts. That is, we come to classify as false some of those sentences that we classified as true when all we were after was to maximize agreement.

[1] e.g. in *Ontological Relativity*, p. 35.

The maxim of maximizing agreement, which we have already modified so as to take into account evidence relations, has to be further supplemented with the evidence we get by observing ostension. In fact, the evidence from ostension has to come first: it should not just be brought in when there is nothing to choose between competing ways of maximizing agreement. When a speaker points in a certain direction, then he should normally be taken to refer to an object which is situated in that direction or to some object related to one of the objects in that direction by deferred ostension.[1] Any satisfactory translation scheme has to allow for this, even to the detriment of agreement.

Of course, not all pointing is ostension—therefore the qualification 'normally', above. To know which cases of pointing are attempts to indicate a reference, we need a theory of action. This brings us to the third kind of evidence we have to consider. We have to combine the study of meaning with a study of human action. This must take place in two ways:

(a) We must take into account that linguistic acts are actions. This includes, for example, the acts of assent and dissent that play such an important role in all the conditions on translation that we have discussed. Such acts involve beliefs and values that one has to take into account in studying language and meaning. Thus, for example, one assumes that what is asserted is, at least in most cases, believed by the asserter to be true. These assumptions are by no means unjustified. Thus, as evidence for the assumption that what is asserted is in most cases believed by the asserter, one could, for example, cite the fact that while a redundancy theory of truth has tempted many, nobody has ever suggested a redundancy theory of falsity. What is important is that we recognize that such assumptions are made.[2]

(b) As we have noted, meaning and belief enter in a number of other areas where language is not used. Prominently, observation of a person's *actions* gives us clues to his values and his beliefs. These clues must fit in with what we assume about his beliefs when we try to translate what he says, and they thereby aid in translation. Note that

---

[1] For the notion of deferred ostension, see Quine, *Ontological Relativity*, pp. 40 ff.

[2] Quine acknowledges that the linguist's decision as to what to treat as native signs of assent and dissent is on a par with the analytical hypotheses in his reply to Hintikka in *Words and Objections*, pp. 312–13.

the connection between a person's beliefs and his actions is by no means simple, as is well known to economists who have been working on the problems of so called 'revealed preference'. The difficulties are mainly the following:

(1) A person's actions depend upon both his beliefs and his values, and these two factors are interdependent, so that our assessments of one of them depend on our assessments of the other. As Donald Davidson has observed (in conversation), this inextricability of value and belief by means of observations of actions is parallel to the inextricability of meaning and belief by means of observations of assent and dissent to sentences.
(2) Not all actions are rational. For example, we often act without having compared the alternatives systematically.
(3) Man is a social animal, and as has been pointed out by Amartya Sen,[1] our choices are not rigidly bound to our own preferences, but are also governed by moral and social rules which will often make our actions deviate from those that would accord with individualistic rational calculus.

Thus, we cannot easily read off a person's beliefs from his actions. However, the assumptions we make concerning a person's beliefs when we seek to explain his actions must fit in with those assumptions we make concerning his beliefs when we translate what he says. The two parallel pairs value/belief and meaning/belief have one element in common, namely belief. In view of this common element, the study of language and the study of action have to go hand in hand. Observations of actions help cut down on indeterminacy of translation, and interpretation of what a person says helps determine his preferences and explain his actions.

I think that the notion of meaning we are after, and that underlies communication, is the joint product of all the evidence available to persons who in their daily life try to communicate. Meaning is not something inscrutable that goes beyond empirical evidence. Here, if anywhere, where the evidence leaves off, there is nothing more to be right or wrong about. Conversely, if one is to know all there is to know about meaning and not leave indeterminate more than need be, one must take into account *all* this evidence. As I have argued, a

[1] Most recently in his inaugural lecture, *Behaviour and the Concept of Preference*, The London School of Economics and Political Science, 1973.

theory of meaning must, therefore, include a theory of the evidence relations that hold between our beliefs and our experience, that is an epistemology and a theory of action. To sum up, any satisfactory theory of meaning must take into account how meaning is connected with the whole variety of human experience.[1]

[1] I am grateful to Samuel Guttenplan and Dennis Matthies for their help in improving my English. I am also grateful to Patrick Suppes for many helpful comments.

3 The First Person

G. E. M. ANSCOMBE

DESCARTES and St. Augustine share not only the argument *Cogito ergo sum*—in Augustine *Si fallor, sum*[1]—but also the corollary argument claiming to prove that *the mind* (Augustine) or, as Descartes puts it, *this I*, is not any kind of body. "I could suppose I had no body," wrote Descartes, "but not that I was not", and inferred that "this I" is not a body. Augustine says "The mind knows itself to think", and "it knows its own substance": hence "it is certain of being that alone, which alone it is certain of being."[2] Augustine is not here explicitly offering an argument in the first person, as Descartes is. The first-person character of Descartes's argument means that each person must administer it to himself in the first person; and the assent to St Augustine's various propositions will equally be made, if at all, by appropriating them in the first person. In these writers there is the assumption that when one says "I" or "the mind", one is naming something such that the knowledge of its existence, which is a knowledge of itself as thinking in all the various modes, determines what it is that is known to exist.

Saul Kripke has tried to reinstate Descartes's argument for his dualism. But he neglects its essentially first-person character, making it an argument about the non-identity of *Descartes* with his own body. Whatever else is said, it seems clear that the argument in Descartes depends on results of applying the method of doubt.[3] But

[1] *De Civitate Dei*, XI. 26.
[2] *De Trinitate*, Book X.
[3] *Principles of Philosophy*, I. LX contains Descartes's best statement, which is I think immune to the usual accusation of substitutional fallacy: "Each of us conceives of himself as a conscious being, and can in thought exclude from himself any other substance, whether conscious or extended; so from this mere fact it is

by that method Descartes must have doubted the existence of the man Descartes: at any rate of that figure in the world of his time, that Frenchman, born of such-and-such a stock and christened René; but also, even of the man—unless a man isn't a sort of animal. *If*, then, the non-identity of himself with his own body follows from his starting-points, so equally does the non-identity of himself with the man Descartes. "I am not Descartes" was just as sound a conclusion for him to draw as "I am not a body." To cast the argument in the third person, replacing "I" by "Descartes", is to miss this. Descartes would have accepted the conclusion. That mundane, practical, every-day sense in which it would have been correct for him to say "I am Descartes" was of no relevance to him in these arguments. That which is named by "I"—*that*, in *his* book, was not *Descartes*.

It may seem strange to say: "The non-identity of himself with Descartes was as valid a conclusion as the other" and not treat this as already a *reductio ad absurdum*. For is that phrase not equivalent to "the non-identity of *Descartes* with Descartes"?

No. It is not. For what is in question is not the ordinary reflexive pronoun, but a peculiar reflexive, which has to be explained in terms of "I". It is the reflexive called by grammarians the 'indirect reflexive' and there are languages (Greek, for example) in which there is a special form for it.[1]

---

certain that each of us, so regarded, is really distinct from every other conscious substance and from every corporeal substance. And even if we supposed that God had conjoined some corporeal substance to such a conscious substance so closely that they could not be more closely joined, and had thus compounded a unity out of the two, yet even so they remain really distinct" (*Philosophical Writings*, trans. G. E. M. Anscombe and P. T. Geach). Rendering Descartes's premise here as "I can conceive myself not to include or be my body", we come close to Kripke's version (but in the first person) "Possibly I am not *A*", where "*A*" means my body. But why can I so conceive myself if not because I can doubt the existence of my body?

But "doubting" here does not mean merely reflecting that I am ignorant of the existence of my body though not of myself. So understood, the argument would indeed involve the substitutional fallacy. "Doubting" means clearly understanding that the existence of my body is not guaranteed by something which is thoroughly understood, and is all I am sure of: the existence of myself. We see the importance of the premise supplied by St. Augustine "The mind knows its own existence."

[1] ἕ, οὗ, οἷ. See Thucydides II. 13. The form is rare. Credit for discerning the indirect reflexive in English, which does not have a distinct form for it, belongs in the present day to H.-N. Castaneda in "The Logic of Self-Knowledge", *Nous*, I (1967), 9–22. But his presentation is excessively complicated and I believe it has not attracted enough attention to the substantive point.

"When John Smith spoke of James Robinson he was speaking of his brother, but he did not know this." That's a possible situation. So similarly is "When John Smith spoke of John Horatio Auberon Smith (named in a will perhaps) he was speaking of himself, but he did not know this." If so, then 'speaking of' or 'referring to' oneself is compatible with not knowing that the object one speaks of is oneself.

Yet we are inclined to think that "It's the word each one uses in speaking of himself" explains what "I" names, or explains "I" as a 'referring expression'. It cannot do so if "He speaks of himself" is compatible with ignorance and we are using the reflexive pronoun, in both cases, in the ordinary way.

Nor can we explain the matter, as we might suppose, by saying " 'I' is the word each one uses when he knowingly and intentionally speaks of himself." For did not Smith knowingly and intentionally speak of Smith? Was not the person he intended to speak of— Smith? and so *was* not the person he intended to speak of—himself?

It may be said: "Not in the relevant sense. We all know you can't substitute every designation of the object he intended to speak of and keep the statement about his intention true." But that is not the answer unless the reflexive pronoun itself is a sufficient indication of the way the object is specified. And that is something the ordinary reflexive pronoun cannot be. Consider: "Smith realizes (fails to realize) the identity of an object he calls 'Smith' with himself." If the reflexive pronoun there is the ordinary one, then it specifies for us who frame or hear the sentence, an object whose identity with the object he calls "Smith" Smith does or doesn't realize: namely the object designated by our subject word "Smith". But that does not tell us what identity Smith himself realizes (or fails to realize). For, as Frege held, there is no path back from reference to sense; any object has many ways of being specified, and in this case, through the peculiarity of the construction, we have succeeded in specifying an object (by means of the subject of our sentence) without specifying any conception under which *Smith's* mind is supposed to latch onto it. For we don't want to say "Smith does not realize the identity of Smith with Smith."

We only have to admit a failure of specification of the intended identity, if we persist in treating the reflexive in "He doesn't realize the identity with himself" as the ordinary reflexive. In practice we have no difficulty at all. We know what we mean Smith doesn't realize. It is: "I am Smith." But if that is how we understand that reflexive, it is not the ordinary one. It is a special one which can be explained only in terms of the first person.

If that is right, the explanation of the word "I" as 'the word which each of us uses to speak of himself' is hardly an explanation!—At least, it is no explanation if that reflexive has in turn to be explained in terms of "I"; and if it is the ordinary reflexive, we are back at square one. We seem to need a sense to be specified for this quasiname "I". To repeat the Frege point: we haven't got this sense just by being told which object a man will be speaking of, whether he knows it or not, when he says "I". Of course that phrase "whether he knows it or not" seems highly absurd. His use of "I" surely guarantees that he does know it! But we have a right to ask *what* he knows; if "I" expresses a way its object is reached by him, what Frege called an "Art des Gegebenseins", we want to know what that way is and how it comes about that the only object reached in that way by anyone is identical with himself.

To say all this is to treat "I" as a sort of proper name. That's what gets us into this jam. Certainly "I" functions syntactically like a name. However, it has been observed not to be a proper name. Now this observation may strike us as obvious enough in a trivial sense. After all, we don't call it a proper noun but a personal *pro*noun. It is at any rate not an ordinary proper name. It could not have a lot of the characteristic use of a proper name. For if it is such, it is one that everyone has, and, worse still, one that each person uses only to refer to that person that he himself is. So it's no use for introducing people to one another, or for calling to someone, or for summoning him. And while it might be used as a signature (like the signature of an aged and doddering parson that I heard of, on someone's marriage lines: Me, Vicar), one would be quite dependent on other clues to the identity of the signatory. If this were the only name anyone had, the situation would be worse than it is for a bank in a Welsh village. These inconveniences are avoided, of course, because there are other more various proper names which people have as well. So the observation that "I" is not a proper name seems to reduce to the triviality that we perhaps would not *call* a word a proper name if everyone had it and used it only to speak of himself.—But is even that true? After all, all Sikhs seem to be called "Singh". So the real difference lies in that one point that each one uses the name "I" only to speak of himself. Is that a ground not to call it a proper name? Certainly to the eyes of our logicians it is a proper name. Are their eyes dim? Or is it really logically a proper name?

Let us ask: is it really true that "I" is only not called a proper name because everyone uses it only to refer to himself? Let us construct a clear case of just such a name. Imagine a society in which everyone is labelled with two names. One appears on their backs and at the top of their chests, and these names, which their bearers cannot see, are various: "*B*" to "*Z*" let us say. The other, "*A*", is stamped on the inside of their wrists, and is the same for everyone. In making reports on people's actions everyone uses the names on their chests or backs if he can see these names or is used to seeing them. Everyone also learns to respond to utterance of the name on his own chest and back in the sort of way and circumstances in which we tend to respond to utterance of our names. Reports on one's own actions, which one gives straight off from observation, are made using the name on the wrist. Such reports are made, not on the basis of observation alone, but also on that of inference and testimony or other information. *B*, for example, derives conclusions expressed by sentences with "*A*" as subject, from other people's statements using "*B*" as subject.

It may be asked: what is meant by "reports on one's own actions"? Let us lay it down that this means, for example, reports issuing from the mouth of *B* on the actions of *B*. That is to say: reports from the mouth of *B* saying that *A* did such-and-such are prima facie verified by ascertaining that *B* did it and are decisively falsified by finding that he did not.

Thus for each person there is one person of whom he has characteristically limited and also characteristically privileged views: except in mirrors he never sees the whole person, and can only get rather special views of what he does see. Some of these are specially good, others specially bad. Of course, a man *B* may sometimes make a mistake through seeing the name "*A*" on the wrist of another, and not realizing it is the wrist of a man whose other name is after all not inaccessible to *B* in the special way in which his own name ("*B*") is.

(It may help some people's imagination if we change the example: instead of these rather inhuman people, we suppose machines that are equipped with scanning devices, are marked with signs in the same way as the people in my story were marked with their names, and are programmed to translate what appears on the screens of their scanners into reports.)

In my story we have a specification of a sign as a name, the same for everyone, but used by each only to speak of himself. How does it compare with "I"?—The first thing to note is that our description does not include self-consciousness on the part of the people who use the name "*A*" as I have described it. They perhaps have no self-consciousness, though each one knows a lot about the object that he (in fact) is; and has a name, the same as everyone else has, which he uses in reports about the object that he (in fact) is.

This—that they have not self-consciousness—may, just for that reason, seem not to be true. *B* is conscious of, that is to say he observes, some of *B*'s activities, that is to say his own. He uses the name "*A*", as does everyone else, to refer to himself. So he is conscious of himself. So he has self-consciousness.

But when we speak of self-consciousness we don't mean that. We mean something manifested by the use of "I" as opposed to "*A*".

Hence we must get to understand self-consciousness. Unsurprisingly, the term dates only from the seventeenth century and derives from philosophy. Getting into ordinary language, it alters, and by the nineteenth century acquires a sense which is pretty irrelevant to the philosophical notion: it comes to mean awkwardness from being troubled by the feeling of being an object of observation by other people. Such a change often happens to philosophical terms.—But this one also gets into psychology and psychiatry, and here its sense is not so far removed from the philosophical one.

The first explanation of self-consciousness that may occur to someone, and what the form of the expression suggests, is this: it is consciousness of a self. A self will be something that some things either have or are. If a thing has it it is something connected with the thing, in virtue of which the thing that has it is able to say, and mean, "I". It is what he calls "I". Being able to mean "I" is thus explained as having the right sort of thing to call "I". The fanciful use of the word, if someone should put a placard "I am only a waxwork" on a wax policeman, or in the label on the bottle in *Alice in Wonderland* "Drink me", is a pretence that the objects in question have (or are) selves. *The self* is not a Cartesian idea, but it may be tacked on to Cartesian Ego theory and is a more consequent development of it than Descartes's identification of 'this I' with his soul. If things are, rather than having, selves, then a self is something, for example a human being, in a special aspect, an aspect which he has as soon as he becomes a 'person'. "I" will then be the name used by each one only for himself (this is a direct reflexive) and precisely in that aspect.

On these views one would explain "self" in "self-consciousness" either by explaining what sort of object that accompanying self was, or by explaining what the aspect was. Given such explanation, one might have that special 'way of being given' of an object which is associated with the name one uses in speaking of it.

Now all this is strictly nonsensical. It is blown up out of a misconstrue of the reflexive pronoun. That it is nonsense comes out also in the following fact: it would be a question what guaranteed that one got hold of the right self, that is, that the self a man called "I" was always connected with *him*, or was always the man himself. Alternatively, if one said that "the self connected with a man" meant just the one he meant by "I" at any time, whatever self that was, it would be by a mere favour of fate that it had anything else to do with him.

But "self-consciousness" is not any such nonsense. It is something real, though as yet unexplained, which "I"-users have and which would be lacking to "*A*"-users, if their use of "*A*" was an adequate tool for their consciousness of themselves.

The expression "self-consciousness" can be respectably explained as 'consciousness that such-and-such holds of oneself'. Nor should we allow an argument running: since the occurrence of "oneself" is just like the occurrence of "himself" which left us perfectly well understanding what Smith failed to realize, the word "self" must itself connote the desired 'way of being given' that is associated with "I" as (logically speaking) a proper name. We must reject this argument because "oneself" is here nothing but the indirect reflexive: that is to say, the reflexive of indirect speech. Understanding indirect speech we know what the related direct speech is. That is all.

These considerations will lack appeal. The question was, what does "I" stand for? If that question is asked, and "I" is supposed to stand for its object as a proper name does, we need an account of a certain kind. The use of a name for an object is connected with a conception of that object. And so we are driven to look for something that, for each "I"-user, will be the conception related to the supposed name "I", as the conception of a city is to the names "London" and "Chicago", that of a river to "Thames" and "Nile", that of a man to "John" and "Pat". Such a conception is requisite if "I" is a name, and there is no conception that can claim to do the job except one suggested by 'self-consciousness'. That is why some philosophers have elaborated the notion of 'selves' (or 'persons' defined in terms of self-consciousness) and conducted investigations to see what such things may be. And just as we must be continuing our reference to the same city if we continue to use "London" with the same reference, so we must each of us be continuing our reference to the same self (or 'person') if we continue to use "I" with the same reference.

This led to an imaginative *tour de force* on the part of Locke: might not the thinking substance which thought the thought "I did it"—the genuine thought of agent-memory—nevertheless be a different thinking substance from the one that could have had the thought: "I am doing it" when the act was done? Thus he detached the identity of the self or 'person' from the identity even of the thinking being which does the actual thinking of the I-thoughts.

Considerations about reflexive pronouns are certainly not going to dam up the flood of inquiries about 'the self' or 'selves', so long as "I" is treated as a name and a correlative term is needed for its type of object. Nevertheless, these are embarrassing credentials for such inquiries. And a self *can* be thought of as what "I" stands for, or indicates, without taking "I" as a proper name. The reasons for considering it as a proper name were two: first, that to the logician's eye it is one, and second, that it seemed to be just like our "*A*" (which was clearly a proper name) except that it expressed 'self-consciousness'. So we tried to explain it as a proper name of a self. Now a lot of people who will have no objection to the talk of 'selves' will yet feel uneasy about calling "I" a proper name of a self or anything else. I assume it was made clear that the different reference in each mouth was not an objection (there is no objection to calling "*A*" a proper name), and so there is some other reason. The reason, I think, is that, so understood, a repeated use of "I" in connection with the same self would have to involve a reidentification of that self. For it is presumably always a use in the presence of its object! There is no objection to the topic of reidentification of selves—it is one of the main interests of the philosophers who write about selves—but this is not any part of the role of "I". The corresponding reidentification *was* involved in the use of "*A*", and that makes an additional difference between them.

So perhaps "I" is not a name but rather another kind of expression indicating 'singular reference'. The logician's conception of the proper name after all only required *this* feature. There are expressions which logically and syntactically function as proper names without being names. Possibly definite descriptions do, and certainly some pronouns. "I" is called a pronoun, so we will consider this first. Unluckily the category 'pronoun' tells us nothing, since a singular pronoun may even be a variable (as in "If anyone says that, *he* is a fool") —and hence not any kind of singular designation of an object. The suggestion of the word "pronoun" itself is not generally borne out by pronouns. Namely, that you get the same sense in a sentence if you replace the pronoun in it by a name, common or proper: what name in particular, it would be difficult to give a general rule for. Perhaps "pronoun" seemed an apt name just for the personal pronouns and especially for "I". But the sense of the lie "I am not E.A." is hardly retained in "E.A. is not E.A." So that suggestion is of little value.

Those singular pronouns called demonstratives ("this" and "that") are a clear example of non-names which function logically as names. For in true propositions containing them they provide reference to a distinctly identifiable subject-term (an object) of which something is predicated. Perhaps, then, "I" is a kind of demonstrative.

Assimilation to a demonstrative will not—as would at one time have been thought—do away with the demand for a conception of the object indicated. For, even though someone may say just "this" or "that", we need to know the answer to the question "this *what*?" if we are to understand him; and he needs to know the answer if he is to be meaning anything.[1]

Thus a singular demonstrative, used correctly, does provide us with a proper logical subject so long as it does not lack a 'bearer' or

[1] This point was not grasped in the days when people believed in pure ostensive definition without the ground's being prepared for it. Thus also in those days it was possible not to be so much impressed as we ought to be, by the fact that we can find no well-accounted-for term corresponding to "I" as "city" does to "London". It was possible to see that there was no 'sense' (in Frege's sense) for "I" as a proper name, but still to think that for each one of us "I" was the proper name of an 'object of acquaintance', a *this*. What *this* was could then be called "a self", and the word "self" would be felt to need no further justification. Thus, for example, McTaggart. See *The Nature of Existence*, Vol. II, ¶¶ 382, 386–7, 390–1, 394.

'referent', and so it conforms to the logician's requirement for a name. And the answer to the question "this what?" might be taken to be "this self", if it can be shewn that there are selves and that they are apparently what is spoken of by all these people saying "I". Thus would these philosophical inquiries about selves have a certain excuse.

It used to be thought that a singular demonstrative, "this" or "that", if used correctly, could not lack a referent. But this is not so, as comes out if we consider the requirement for an answer to "this what?". Someone comes with a box and says "This is all that is left of poor Jones." The answer to "this what?" is "this parcel of ashes"; but unknown to the speaker the box is empty. What "this" has to have, if used correctly, is something that it *latches on to* (as I will put it): in this example it is the box. In another example it might be an optical presentation. Thus I may ask "What's that figure standing in front of the rock, a man or a post?" and there may be no such object at all; but there is an appearance, a stain perhaps, or other marking of the rock face, which my "that" latches on to. The referent and what "this" latches on to may coincide, as when I say "this buzzing in my ears is dreadful", or, after listening to a speech, "That was splendid!" But they do not have to coincide, and the referent is the object of which the predicate is predicated where "this" or "that" is a subject.

There is no other pronoun but a demonstrative to which "I" could plausibly be assimilated as a singular term that provides a reference. Of course someone may say: "Why assimilate it at all? Each thing is what it is and not another thing! So "I" is a pronoun all right, but it is merely the pronoun that it is." But that is no good, because 'pronoun' is just a rag-bag category; one might as well say: "it is the word that it is." The problem is to describe its meaning. And, if its meaning involves the idea of reference, to see what 'reference' is here, and how accomplished. We are now supposing that it is not accomplished as it is for a regular proper name; then, if "I" is not an abbreviation of a definite description, it must catch hold of its object in some other way—and what way is there but the demonstrative?

But there is a contrast between "I" and the ordinary demonstrative. We saw that there may be reference-failure for "this", in that one may mean "this parcel of ashes" when there are no ashes. But "I"—

if it makes a reference, if, that is, its mode of meaning is that it is supposed to make a reference—is secure against reference-failure. Just thinking "I . . ." guarantees not only the existence but the presence of its referent. It guarantees the existence *because* it guarantees the presence, which is presence to consciousness. But N.B., here "presence to consciousness" means physical or real presence, not just that one is thinking of the thing. For if the thinking did not guarantee the presence, the existence of the referent could be doubted. For the same reason, if "I" is a name it cannot be an empty name. I's existence is existence in the thinking of the thought expressed by "I . . ." This of course is the point of the *cogito*—and, I will show, of the corollary argument too.

Whether "I" is a name or a demonstrative, there is the same need of a 'conception' through which it attaches to its object. Now what conception can be suggested, other than that of *thinking*, the thinking of the I-thought, which secures this guarantee against reference-failure? It may be very well to describe what selves are; but if I do not know that I am a self, then I cannot mean a self by "I".

To point this up, let me imagine a logician, for whom the syntactical character of "I" as a proper name is quite sufficient to guarantee it as such, and for whom the truth of propositions with it as subject is therefore enough to guarantee the existence of the object it names. He, of course, grants all that I have pointed out about the indirect reflexive. It cannot perturb him, so long as the 'way of being given' is of no concern to him. To him it is clear that "I", in my mouth, is just another name for E.A. "I" may have some curious characteristics; but they don't interest him. The reason is that "I" is a name governed by the following rule:

If *X* makes assertions with "I" as subject, then those assertions will be true if and only if the predicates used thus assertively are true of *X*.

This will be why Kripke—and others discussing Descartes—make the transition from Descartes's "I" to "Descartes".

Now first, this offers too swift a refutation of Descartes. In order to infer straight away that Descartes was wrong, we only need the information that Descartes asserted "I am not a body", together with the knowledge that he was a man: that is, an animal of a certain species; that is, a body living with a certain sort of life.

But there would and should come from Descartes's lips or pen a denial that, strictly speaking, *the man Descartes* made the assertion. The rule was sound enough. But the asserting subject must be the thinking subject. If you are a speaker who says "I", you do not find out what is saying "I". You do not for example look to see what apparatus the noise comes out of and assume that that is the sayer; or frame the hypothesis of something connected with it that is the sayer. If that were in question, you could doubt whether anything *was* saying "I". As, indeed, you can doubt whether anything is saying it out loud. (And sometimes *that* doubt is correct.)

Thus we need to press our logician about the 'guaranteed reference' of "I". In granting this, there are three degrees of it that he may assert. (1) He may say that of course the user of "I" must exist, otherwise he would not be using "I". As he *is* the referent, that is what 'guaranteed reference' amounts to. In respect of such guaranteed reference, he may add, there will be no difference between "I" and "*A*". But the question is, why "I" was said to *refer* to the "I"-user? Our logician held that "I" was logically a proper name—a singular term whose role is to make a reference—for two reasons: one, that "I" has the same syntactical place as such expressions, and the other, that it can be replaced *salva veritate* by a (more ordinary) name of *X* when it occurs in subject position in assertions made by *X*. In saying this, he no doubt thought himself committed to no views on the sense of "I" or what the "I"-user means by "I". But his second reason amounts to this: one who hears or reads a statement with "I" as subject needs to know whose statement it is if he wants to know of whom the predicate holds if the statement is true. Now, this requirement could be signalled by flashing a green light, say, in connection with the predicate, or perhaps adding a terminal '-O' to it. (I apologize to anyone who finds this suggestion altogether too fanciful, and beg him to suspend disbelief.) What would make such a signal or suffix into a referring expression? The essential argument cannot be an argument back from syntax to reference, for such an argument would depend only on the form of sentence and would be absurd. (e.g. no one thinks that "it is raining" contains a referring expression, "it".) And so it seems that our logician cannot disclaim concern with the sense of "I", or at any rate with what the "I"-user must mean.

(2) So the "I"-user must intend to refer to something, if "I" is a

referring expression. And now there are two different things for "guaranteed reference" to mean here. It may mean (2a) guaranteed existence of the object meant by the user. That is to say, that object must exist, which he is taking something to be when he uses the expression in connection with it. Thus, if I suppose I know someone called "*X*" and I call something "*X*" with the intention of referring to that person, a guarantee of reference in this sense would be a guarantee that there is such a thing as *X*. The name "*A*" which I invented would have this sort of guaranteed reference. The "*A*"-user means to speak of a certain human being, one who falls under his observation in a rather special way. That person is himself, and so, given that he has grasped the use of "*A*", he cannot but be speaking of a real person.

If our logician takes this as an adequate account of the guaranteed reference of "I", then he will have to grant that there is a further sort of 'guaranteed reference', which "I" does *not* have. Guaranteed reference for that name "*X*" in this further sense (2b) would entail a guarantee, not just that there is such a thing as *X*, but also that what I take to be *X is X*. We saw that the "*A*"-user would not be immune to mistaken identification of someone else as '*A*'. Will it also be so with "I"?

The suggestion seems absurd. It seems clear that if "I" is a 'referring expression' at all, it has both kinds of guaranteed reference. The object an "I"-user means by it must exist so long as he is using "I", nor can he take the wrong object to be the object he means by "I". (The bishop may take the lady's knee for his, but could he take the lady herself to be himself?)

Let us waive the question about the sense of "I" and ask *only* how reference to the right object could be guaranteed. (This is appropriate, because people surely have here the idea of a sort of pure direct reference in which one simply first means and then refers to an object before one.) It seems, then, that this reference could only be sure-fire if the referent of "I" were both freshly defined with each use of "I", and also remained in view so long as something was being taken to be *I*. Even so there is an assumption that something else does not surreptitiously take its place. Perhaps we should say: such an assumption is extremely safe for "I", and it would be altogether an excess of scepticism to doubt it! So we accept the assumption, and it seems to follow that what "I" stands for must be a Cartesian Ego.

For, let us suppose that it is some other object. A plausible one would be *this body*. And now imagine that I get into a state of 'sensory deprivation'. Sight is cut off, and I am locally anaesthetized everywhere, perhaps floated in a tank of tepid water; I am unable to speak, or to touch any part of my body with any other. Now I tell myself "I won't let this happen again!" If the object meant by "I" is this body, this human being, then in these circumstances it won't be present to my senses; and how else can it be 'present to' me? But have I lost what I mean by "I"? Is that not present to me? Am I reduced to, as it were, 'referring in absence'? I have not lost my 'self-consciousness'; nor can what I mean by "I" be an object no longer present to me. This both seems right in itself, and will be required by the 'guaranteed reference' that we are considering.

Like considerations will operate for other suggestions. Nothing but a Cartesian Ego will serve. Or, rather, a stretch of one. People have sometimes queried how Descartes could conclude to his RES *cogitans*.[1] But this is to forget that Descartes declares its essence to be nothing but thinking. The thinking that thinks this thought—that is what is guaranteed by "cogito".

Thus we discover that *if* "I" is a referring expression, then Descartes was right about what the referent was. His position has, however, the intolerable difficulty of requiring an identification of the same referent in different "I"-thoughts. (This led Russell at one point to speak of 'short-term selves'.)

Our questions were a combined *reductio ad absurdum* of the idea of "I" as a word whose role is to 'make a singular reference'. I mean the questions how one is guaranteed to get the object right, whether one may safely assume no unnoticed substitution, whether one could refer to oneself 'in absence', and so on. The suggestion of getting the object right collapses into absurdity when we work it out and try to describe how getting hold of the wrong object may be excluded.

How, even, could one justify the assumption, if it is an assumption, that there is just one thinking which is this thinking of this thought that I am thinking, just one thinker? How do I know that 'I' is not ten thinkers thinking in unison? Or perhaps not quite succeeding. That might account for the confusion of thought which I sometimes feel.—Consider the reply "Legion, for we are many", given by the possessed man in the gospel. Perhaps we should take that solemnly,

---

[1] A. J. Ayer for example. See *Language, Truth and Logic*, p. 142.

not as a grammatical joke.[1]—These considerations refute the 'definite description' account of "I". For the only serious candidate for such an account is "The sayer of this", where "sayer" implies "thinker". Getting hold of the wrong object *is* excluded, and that makes us think that getting hold of the right object is guaranteed. But the reason is that there is no getting hold of an object at all. With names, or denoting expressions (in Russell's sense) there are two things to grasp: the kind of use, and what to apply them to from time to time. With "I" there is only the use.

If this is too hard to believe, if "I" *is* a 'referring expression', then Descartes was right. But now the troubles start. At first, it seems as if what "I" stands for ought to be the clearest and certainest thing— what anyone thinking of his own thinking and his own awareness of anything is most evidently aware of. It is most certain because, as Augustine said, it is involved in the knowledge of all mental acts or states by the one who has them. They could not be doubted. But the *I*, the 'mind', the 'self', was their subject, not their object, and looking for it as an object resulted, some people thought, in total failure. It was not to be found. It was rather as it were an area of darkness out of which light shone on everything else. So some racked their brains over what this invisible subject and the 'thinking of *it*' could be; others thought there was no such thing, there were just all the objects, and hence that "I", rather, was the name of the whole collection of perceptions. But that hardly fitted its grammar, and anyway—a problem which utterly stumped Hume—by what was *I* made into a unity? Others in effect treat selves as postulated objects for "I" to be names of in different people's mouths. Yet others denied that the self was invisible, and claimed that there is a unique feeling of oneself which is indescribable but very, very important, especially in psychology, in clinical psychology, and psychiatry.

With that thought: "The *I* was subject, not object, and hence invisible", we have an example of language itself being as it were possessed of an imagination, forcing its image upon us.

[1] Ambrose Bierce has a pleasant entry under "I" in the *Devil's Dictionary*: "I is the first letter of the alphabet, the first word of the language, the first thought of the mind, the first object of the affections. In grammar it is a pronoun of the first person and singular number. Its plural is said to be *We*, but how there can be more than one myself is doubtless clearer to the grammarians than it is to the author of this incomparable dictionary. Conception of two myselves is difficult, but fine. The frank yet graceful use of "I" distinguishes a good author from a bad; the latter carries it with the manner of a thief trying to cloak his loot."

The dispute is self-perpetuating, endless, irresoluble, so long as we adhere to the initial assumption, made so far by all the parties to it: that "I" is a referring expression. So long as that is the assumption you will get the deep division between those whose considerations show that they have not perceived the difficulty—for them "I" is in principle no different from my "*A*"; and those who do—or would—perceive the difference and are led to rave in consequence.

And this is the solution: "I" is neither a name nor another kind of expression whose logical role is to make a reference, *at all*.

Of course we must accept the rule "If *X* asserts something with 'I' as subject, his assertion will be true if and only if what he asserts is true of *X*." But if someone thinks that is a sufficient account of "I", we must say "No, it is not", for it does not make any difference between "I" and "*A*". The truth-condition of the whole sentence does not determine the meaning of the items within the sentence. Thus the rule does not justify the idea that "I", coming out of *X*'s mouth, is another name for *X*. Or for anything else, such as an asserting subject who is speaking through *X*.

But the rule does mean that the question "*Whose* assertion?" is all-important. And, for example, an interpreter might repeat the "I" of his principal in his translations. Herein resides the conceivability of the following: someone stands before me and says, "Try to believe this: when I say "I", that does not mean this human being who is making the noise. I am someone else who has borrowed this human being to speak through him." When I say "conceivability" I don't mean that such a communication might be the truth, but only that our imagination makes something of the idea. (Mediums, possession.)

If I am right in my general thesis, there is an important consequence —namely, that "I am E.A." is after all not an identity proposition. It is connected with an identity proposition, namely, "This thing here is E.A." But there is also the proposition "I am this thing here".

When a man does not know his identity, has, as we say, 'lost his memory', what he doesn't know is usually that *that* person he'd point to in pointing to himself (this is the direct reflexive) is, say, Smith, a man of such-and-such a background. He has neither lost the use of "I", nor is he usually at a loss what to point to as his body, or as the person he is; nor would he point to an unexpected body, to a stone, a horse, or another man, say. The last two of these three points may seem to be part of the first of them; but, as we have seen, it is possible at least for the imagination to make a division. Note that when I use the word "person" here, I use it in the sense in which it occurs in "offences against the person". At this point people will betray how deeply they are infected by dualism, they will say: "You are using 'person' in the sense of 'body' "—and what *they* mean by "body" is something that is still there when someone is dead. But that is to misunderstand "offences against the person". None such can be committed against a corpse. 'The person' is a living human body.

There is a real question: with what object is my consciousness of action, posture, and movement, and are my intentions connected in such fashion that *that* object must be standing up if I have the thought that I am standing up and my thought is true? And there is an answer to that: it is this object here.

"I am this thing here" is, then, a real proposition, but not a proposition of identity. It means: this thing here is the thing, the person (in the 'offences against the person' sense) of whose action *this* idea of action is an idea, of whose movements *these* ideas of movement are ideas, of whose posture *this* idea of posture is the idea. And also, of which *these* intended actions, if carried out, will be the actions.

I have from time to time such thoughts as "I am sitting", "I am writing", "I am going to stay still", "I twitched". There is the question: in happenings, events, etc. concerning what object are these verified or falsified? The answer is ordinarily easy to give because I can observe, and can point to, my body; I can also feel one part of it with another. "This body is my body" then means "My idea that I am standing up is verified by this body, if it is standing up." And so on. But observation does not show me which body is the one. Nothing shows me that.[1]

If I were in that condition of 'sensory deprivation', I could not have the thought "this object", "this body"—there would be nothing for "this" to latch on to. But that is not to say I could not still have the ideas of actions, motion, etc. For these ideas are not extracts from sensory observation. If I do have them under sensory deprivation, I

[1] Prof. Føllesdal and Mr. Guttenplan tell me that there is some likeness between what I say and what Spinoza says. I am grateful for the observation; but cannot say I understand Spinoza.

shall perhaps *believe* that there is such a body. But the possibility will perhaps strike me that there is none. That is, the possibility that there is then nothing that I am.

If "I" were a name, it would have to be a name for something with this sort of connection with this body, not an extra-ordinary name for this body. Not a name for this body because sensory deprivation and even loss of consciousness of posture, etc., is not loss of *I*. (That, at least, is how one would have to put it, treating "I" as a name.)

But "I" is not a name: these I-thoughts are examples of reflective consciousness of states, actions, motions, etc., not of an object I mean by "I", but of this body. These I-thoughts (allow me to pause and think some!) . . . are unmediated conceptions (knowledge or belief, true or false) of states, motions, etc., of this object here, about which I can find out (if I don't know it) that it is E.A. About which I did learn that it is a human being.

The I-thoughts *now* that have *this* connection with E.A. are I-thoughts on the part of the same human being as the I-thoughts that had that connection twenty years ago. No problem of the continuity or reidentification of 'the *I*' can arise. There is no such thing. There is E.A., who, like other humans, has such thoughts as these. And who probably learned to have them through learning to say what she had done, was doing, etc.—an amazing feat of imitation.

Discontinuity of 'self-feeling', dissociation from the self-feeling or self-image one had before, although one still has memories—such a thing is of course possible. And so perhaps is a loss of self-feeling altogether. What this 'self-feeling' is is no doubt of psychological interest. The more normal state is the absence of such discontinuity, dissociation, and loss. That absence can therefore be called the possession of 'self-feeling': I record my suspicion that this is identifiable rather by consideration of the abnormal than the normal case.

Self-knowledge is knowledge of the object that one is, of the human animal that one is. 'Introspection' is but one contributory method. It is a rather doubtful one, as it may consist rather in the elaboration of a self-image than in noting facts about oneself.

If the principle of human rational life in E.A. is a soul (which perhaps can survive E.A., perhaps again animate E.A.) *that* is not the reference of "I". Nor is it what I am. I am E.A. and shall exist only as long as E.A. exists. But, to repeat, "I am E.A." is not an identity proposition.

It will have been noticeable that the I-thoughts I've been considering have been only those relating to actions, postures, movements and intentions. Not, for example, such thoughts as "I have a headache", "I am thinking about thinking", "I see a variety of colours", "I hope, fear, love, envy, desire", and so on. My way is the opposite of Descartes's. These are the very propositions he would have considered, and the others were a difficulty for him. But what were most difficult for him are most easy for me.

Let me repeat what I said before. I have thoughts like "I am standing", "I jumped." It is, I said, a significant question: "In happenings, events, etc., concerning what object are these verified or falsified?"—and the answer was: "this one". The reason why I take only thoughts of actions, postures, movements, and intended actions is that only those thoughts both are unmediated, non-observational, and also are descriptions (e.g. "standing") which are directly verifiable or falsifiable about the person of E.A. Anyone, including myself, can look and see whether that person is standing.

That question "In happenings, events, etc., concerning what object are these verified or falsified?" could indeed be raised about the other, the Cartesianly preferred, thoughts. I should contend that the true answer would be "If in any happenings, events, etc., then in ones concerning this object"—namely the person of E.A. But the description of the happenings, etc., would not be just the same as the description of the thought. I mean the thought "I am standing" is verified by the fact that this person here is *standing*, falsified if she is not. This identity of description is entirely missing for, say, the thought "I see a variety of colours." Of course you may say, if you like, that this is verified if this person here sees a variety of colours, but the question is, what is it for it to be so verified? The Cartesianly preferred thoughts all have this same character, of being far removed in their descriptions from the descriptions of the proceedings, etc., of a person in which they might be verified. And also, there might not be any. And also, even when there are any, the thoughts are not thoughts of such proceedings, as the thought of standing is the thought of a posture. I cannot offer an investigation of these questions here. I only want to indicate why I go after the particular

"I"-thoughts that I do, in explaining the meaning of "I am E.A." This may suffice to show why I think the Cartesianly preferred thoughts are not the ones to investigate if one wants to understand "I" philosophically.

Suppose—as is possible—that there were no distinct first-person expression, no pronoun "I", not even any first-person inflection of verbs. Everyone uses his own name as we use "I". (Children sometimes do this.) Thus a man's own name takes the place of "I" in this supposed language. What then? Won't his own name still be a name? Surely it will! He will be using what is syntactically *and* semantically a name. That is, it is semantically a name in other people's mouths. But it will not be so in his mouth, it will not signify like a name in his utterances.

If I used "E.A." like that, and had no first-person inflections of verbs and no such word as "I", I should be in a difficulty to frame the proposition corresponding to my present proposition: "I am E.A." The nearest I could get would be, for example, "E.A. is the object E.A." That is, "E.A. is the object referred to by people who identify something as E.A."

There is a mistake that it is very easy to make here. It is that of supposing that the difference of self-consciousness, the difference I have tried to bring before your minds as that between "I"-users and "*A*"-users, is a private experience. That there is this asymmetry about "I": for the hearer or reader it is in principle no different from "*A*"; for the speaker or thinker, the "I"-saying subject, it is different. Now this is not so: the difference between "I"-users and "*A*"-users would be perceptible to observers. To bring this out, consider the following story from William James. James, who insisted (rightly, if I am right) that consciousness is quite distinct from self-consciousness, reproduces an instructive letter from a friend: "We were driving . . . in a wagonette; the door flew open and X, alias 'Baldy', fell out on the road. We pulled up at once, and then he said 'Did anyone fall out?' or 'Who fell out?'—I don't exactly remember the words. When told that Baldy fell out he said 'Did Baldy fall out? Poor Baldy!' "[1]

If we met people who were *A*-users and had no other way of speaking of themselves, we would notice it quite quickly, just as his companions noticed what was wrong with Baldy. It was not that he used

[1] *Principles of Psychology*, Vol. II, p. 273 n.

his own name. That came afterwards. What instigated someone to give information to him in the form "Baldy fell out" was, I suppose, that his behaviour already showed the lapse of self-consciousness, as James called it. He had just fallen out of the carriage, he was conscious, and he had the idea that someone had fallen out of the carriage—or he knew that someone had, but wondered who! That was the indication of how things were with him.

Even if they had spoken a language without the word "I", even if they had had one without any first-person inflexion,[1] but everybody used his own name in his expressions of self-consciousness, even so, Baldy's conduct would have had just the same significance. It wasn't that he used 'Baldy' and not "I" in what he said. It was that his thought of the happening, falling out of the carriage, was one for which he looked for a subject, his grasp of it one which required a subject. And that could be explained even if we didn't have "I" or distinct first-person inflexions. He did not have what I will call 'unmediated agent-or-patient conceptions of actions, happenings, and states'. These conceptions are subjectless. That is, they do not involve the connection of what is understood by a predicate with a distinctly conceived subject. The (deeply rooted) grammatical illusion of a subject is what generates all the errors which we have been considering.

POST SCRIPTUM: My colleague Dr. J. Altham has pointed out to me a difficulty about the rule about "I" on page 55. How is one to extract the *predicate* for purposes of this rule in "I think John loves me"? The rule needs supplementation: where "I" or "me" occurs within an oblique context, the predicate is to be specified by replacing "I" or "me" by the indirect reflexive pronoun.

[1] In Latin we have "ambulo" = "I walk". There is no subject-term. There is no need of one.

4 The Nature of Natural Knowledge[1]

W. V. QUINE

DOUBT has oft been said to be the mother of philosophy. This has a true ring for those of us who look upon philosophy primarily as the theory of knowledge. For the theory of knowledge has its origin in doubt, in scepticism. Doubt is what prompts us to try to develop a theory of knowledge. Furthermore, doubt is also the first step to take in developing a theory of knowledge, if we adopt the line of Descartes.

But this is only half of a curious interplay between doubt and knowledge. Doubt prompts the theory of knowledge, yes; but knowledge, also, was what prompted the doubt. Scepticism is an offshoot of science. The basis for scepticism is the awareness of illusion, the discovery that we must not always believe our eyes. Scepticism battens on mirages, on seemingly bent sticks in water, on rainbows, after-images, double images, dreams. But in what sense are these illusions? In the sense that they seem to be material objects which they in fact are not. Illusions are illusions only relative to a prior acceptance of genuine bodies with which to contrast them. In a world of immediate sense data with no bodies posited and no questions asked, a distinction between reality and illusion would have no place. The positing of bodies is already rudimentary physical science; and it is only after that stage that the sceptic's invidious distinctions can make sense. Bodies have to be posited before there can be a motive, however tenuous, for acquiescing in a non-committal world of the immediate given.

Rudimentary physical science, that is, common sense about bodies,

[1] This paper is meant as a summary statement of my attitude towards our knowledge of nature. Consequently I must warn the more omnivorous of my readers (dear souls) that they are apt to experience a certain indefinable sense of *déjà lu*. The main traces of novelty come towards the end.

is thus needed as a springboard for scepticism. It contributes the needed notion of a distinction between reality and illusion, and that is not all. It also discerns regularities of bodily behaviour which are indispensable to that distinction. The sceptic's example of the seemingly bent stick owes its force to our knowledge that sticks do not bend by immersion; and his examples of mirages, after-images, dreams, and the rest are similarly parasitic upon positive science, however primitive.

I am not accusing the sceptic of begging the question. He is quite within his rights in assuming science in order to refute science; this, if carried out, would be a straightforward argument by *reductio ad absurdum*. I am only making the point that sceptical doubts are scientific doubts.

Epistemologists have coped with their sceptical doubts by trying to reconstruct our knowledge of the external world from sensations. A characteristic effort was Berkeley's theory of vision, in which he sought our clues for a third dimension, depth, in our two-dimensional visual field. The very posing of this epistemological problem depends in a striking way upon acceptations of physical science. The goal of the construction, namely the depth dimension, is of course deliberately taken from the science of the external world; but what particularly wants noticing is that also the accepted basis of the construction, the two-dimensional visual field, was itself dictated by the science of the external world as well. The light that informs us of the external world impinges on the two-dimensional surface of the eye, and it was Berkeley's awareness of this that set his problem.

Epistemology is best looked upon, then, as an enterprise within natural science. Cartesian doubt is not the way to begin. Retaining our present beliefs about nature, we can still ask how we can have arrived at them. Science tells us that our only source of information about the external world is through the impact of light rays and molecules upon our sensory surfaces. Stimulated in these ways, we somehow evolve an elaborate and useful science. How do we do this, and why does the resulting science work so well? These are genuine questions, and no feigning of doubt is needed to appreciate them. They are scientific questions about a species of primates, and they are open to investigation in natural science, the very science whose acquisition is being investigated.

The utility of science, from a practical point of view, lies in fulfilled expectation: true prediction. This is true not only of sophisticated science, but of its primitive progenitor as well; and it may be good strategy on our part to think first of the most primitive case. This case is simple induction. It is the expectation, when some past event recurs, that the sequel of that past event will recur too. People are prone to this, and so are other animals.

It may be felt that I am unduly intellectualizing the dumb animals in attributing expectation and induction to them. Still the net resultant behaviour of dumb animals is much on a par with our own, at the level of simple induction. In a dog's experience, a clatter of pans in the kitchen has been followed by something to eat. So now, hearing the clatter again, he goes to the kitchen in expectation of dinner. His going to the kitchen is our evidence of his expectation, if we care to speak of expectation. Or we can skip this intervening variable, as Skinner calls it, and speak merely of reinforced response, conditioned reflex, habit formation.

When we talk easily of repetition of events, repetition of stimuli, we cover over a certain significant factor. It is the *similarity* factor. It can be brought into the open by speaking of events rather as unique, dated, unrepeated particulars, and then speaking of similarities between them. Each of the noisy episodes of the pans is a distinct event, however similar, and so is each of the ensuing dinners. What we can say of the dog in those terms is that he hears something similar to the old clatter and proceeds to expect something similar to the old dinner. Or, if we want to eliminate the intervening variable, we can still say this: when the dog hears something similar to the old clatter and, going to the kitchen, gets something similar to the old dinner, he is reinforced in his disposition to go to the kitchen after each further event similar to the old clatter.

What is significant about this similarity factor is its subjectivity. Is similarity the mere sharing of many attributes? But any two things share countless attributes—or anyway any two objects share membership in countless classes. The similarity that matters, in the clatter of the pans, is similarity for the dog. Again I seem to appeal to the dog's mental life, but again I can eliminate this intervening variable. We can analyse similarity, for the dog, in terms of his dispositions to behaviour: his patterns of habit formation. His habit of going to the kitchen after a clatter of pans is itself our basis for saying that the clatter events are similar for the dog, and that the dinner events are similar for the dog. It is by experimental reinforcement and extinction along these lines that we can assess similarities for the dog, determining whether event *a* is more similar to *b* than to *c* for him. Meanwhile his mental life is as may be.

Now our question 'Why is science so successful?' makes some rudimentary sense already at this level, as applied to the dog. For the dog's habit formation, his primitive induction, involved extrapolation along similarity lines: episodes similar to the old clattering episode engendered expectation of episodes similar to the old dinner episode. And now the crux of the problem is the subjectivity of similarity. Why should nature, however lawful, match up at all with the dog's subjective similarity ratings? Here, at its most primitive, is the question 'Why is science so successful?'

We are taking this as a scientific question, remember, open to investigation by natural science itself. Why should the dog's implicit similarity ratings tend to fit world trends, in such a way as to favour the dog's implicit expectations? An answer is offered by Darwin's theory of natural selection. Individuals whose similarity groupings conduce largely to true expectations have a good chance of finding food and avoiding predators, and so a good chance of living to reproduce their kind.

What I have said of the dog holds equally of us, at least in our pursuit of the rudimentary science of common sense. We predict in the light of observed uniformities, and these are uniformities by our subjective similarity standards. These standards are innate ones, overlaid and modified by experience; and natural selection has endowed us, like the dog, with a head start in the way of helpful, innate similarity standards.

I am not appealing to Darwinian biology to justify induction. This would be circular, since biological knowledge depends on induction. Rather I am granting the efficacy of induction, and then observing that Darwinian biology, if true, helps explain why induction is as efficacious as it is.

We must notice, still, a further limitation. Natural selection may be expected only to have encouraged similarity standards conducive to rough and ready anticipations of experience in a state of nature. Such standards are not necessarily conducive to deep science. Colour is a case in point. Colour dominates our scene; similarity in colour is similarity at its most conspicuous. Yet, as J. J. C. Smart points out, colour plays little role in natural science. Things can be alike in colour even though one of them is reflecting green light of uniform wave length while the other is reflecting mixed waves of yellow and blue. Properties that are most germane to sophisticated science are camouflaged by colour more than revealed by it. Over-sensitivity to colour may have been all to the good when we were bent on quickly distinguishing predator from prey or good plants from bad. But true science cuts through all this and sorts things out differently, leaving colour largely irrelevant.

Colour is not the only such case. Taxonomy is rich in examples to show that visual resemblance is a poor index of kinship. Natural selection has even abetted the deception; thus some owls have grown to resemble cats, for their own good, and others resemble monkeys. Natural selection works both to improve a creature's similarity standards and to help him abuse his enemies' similarity standards.

For all their fallibility, our innate similarity standards are indispensable to science as an entering wedge. They continue to be indispensable, moreover, even as science advances. For the advance of science depends on continued observation, continued checking of predictions. And there, at the observational level, the unsophisticated similarity standards of common sense remain in force.

An individual's innate similarity standards undergo some revision, of course, even at the common-sense level, indeed even at the subhuman level, through learning. An animal may learn to tell a cat from an owl. The ability to learn is itself a product of natural selection, with evident survival value. An animal's innate similarity standards are a rudimentary instrument for prediction, and then learning is a progressive refinement of that instrument, making for more dependable prediction. In man, and most conspicuously in recent centuries, this refinement has consisted in the development of a vast and bewildering growth of conceptual or linguistic apparatus, the whole of natural science. Biologically, still, it is like the animal's learning about cats and owls; it is a learned improvement over simple induction by innate similarity standards. It makes for more and better prediction.

Science revises our similarity standards, we saw; thus we discount colour, for some purposes, and we liken whales to cows rather than to fish. But this is not the sole or principal way in which science fosters prediction. Mere improvement of similarity standards would increase our success at simple induction, but this is the least of it. Science departs from simple induction. Science is a ponderous linguistic structure, fabricated of theoretical terms linked by fabricated hypotheses, and keyed to observable events here and there. Indirectly, via this labyrinthine superstructure, the scientist predicts future observations on the basis of past ones; and he may revise the super-structure when the predictions fail. It is no longer simple induction. It is the hypothetico-deductive method. But, like the animal's simple induction over innate similarities, it is still a biological device for anticipating experience. It owes its elements still to natural selection —notably, the similarity standards that continue to operate at the observational level. The biological survival value of the resulting scientific structure, however, is as may be. Traits that were developed by natural selection have been known to prove lethal, through over-development or remote effects or changing environment. In any event, and for whatever good it may do us, the hypothetico-deductive method is delivering knowledge hand over fist. It is facilitating pre-diction.

I said that science is a linguistic structure that is keyed to observa-tion at some points. Some sentences are keyed directly to observa-tion: the observation sentences. Let us examine this connection. First I must explain what I mean by an observation sentence. One dis-tinctive trait of such a sentence is that its truth value varies with the circumstances prevailing at the time of the utterance. It is a sentence like 'This is red' or 'It is raining', which is true on one occasion and false on another; unlike 'Sugar is sweet', whose truth value endures regardless of occasion of utterance. In a word, observation sentences are occasion sentences, not standing sentences.

But their being occasion sentences is not the only distinctive trait of observation sentences. Not only must the truth value of an ob-servation sentence depend on the circumstances of its utterance; it must depend on intersubjectively observable circumstances. Cer-tainly the fisherman's sentence 'I just felt a nibble' is true or false depending on the circumstances of its utterance; but the relevant circumstances are privy to the speaker rather than being out in the open for all present witnesses to share. The sentence 'I just felt a nibble' is an occasion sentence but not an observation sentence, in my sense of the term.

An observation sentence, then, is an occasion sentence whose occasion is intersubjectively observable. But this is still not enough. After all, the sentence 'There goes John's old tutor' meets these re-quirements; it is an occasion sentence, and all present witnesses can see the old tutor plodding by. But the sentence fails of a third require-ment: the witnesses must in general be able to appreciate that the observation which they are sharing is one that verifies the sentence.

They must have been in a position, equally with the speaker, to have assented to the sentence on their own in the circumstances. They are in that position in the case of 'This is red' and 'It is raining' and 'There goes an old man', but not in the case of 'There goes John's old tutor.'

Such, then, is an observation sentence: it is an occasion sentence whose occasion is not only intersubjectively observable but is generally adequate, moreover, to elicit assent to the sentence from any present witness conversant with the language. It is not a report of private sense data; typically, rather, it contains references to physical objects.

These sentences, I say, are keyed directly to observation. But how *keyed*, now—what is the nature of the connection? It is a case of conditioned response. It is not quite the simplest kind; we do not say 'red' or 'This is red' whenever we see something red. But we do assent if asked. Mastery of the term 'red' is acquisition of the habit of assenting when the term is queried in the presence of red, and only in the presence of red.

At the primitive level, an observation sentence is apt to take the form of a single word, thus 'ball', or 'red'. What makes it easy to learn is the intersubjective observability of the relevant circumstances at the time of utterance. The parent can verify that the child is seeing red at the time, and so can reward the child's assent to the query. Also the child can verify that the parent is seeing red when the parent assents to such a query.

In this habit formation the child is in effect determining, by induction, the range of situations in which the adult will assent to the query 'red', or approve the child's utterance of 'red'. He is extrapolating along similarity lines; this red episode is similar to that red episode by his lights. His success depends, therefore, on substantial agreement between his similarity standards and those of the adult. Happily the agreement holds; and no wonder, since our similarity standards are a matter partly of natural selection and partly of subsequent experience in a shared environment. If substantial agreement in similarity standards were not there, this first step in language acquisition would be blocked.

We have been seeing that observation sentences are the starting-points in the learning of language. Also, they are the starting-points and the check points of scientific theory. They serve both purposes for one and the same reason: the intersubjective observability of the relevant circumstances at the time of utterance. It is this, inter-subjective observability at the time, that enables the child to learn when to assent to the observation sentence. And it is this also, inter-subjective observability at the time, that qualifies observation sentences as check points for scientific theory. Observation sentences state the evidence, to which all witnesses must accede.

I had characterized science as a linguistic structure that is keyed to observation at some points. Now we have seen how it is keyed to observation: some of the sentences, the observation sentences, are conditioned to observable events in combination with a routine of query and assent. There is the beginning, here, of a partnership between the theory of language learning and the theory of scientific evidence. It is clear, when you think about it, that this partnership must continue. For when a child learns his language from his elders, what has he to go on? He can learn observation sentences by consideration of their observable circumstances, as we saw. But how can he learn the rest of the language, including the theoretical sentences of science? Somehow he learns to carry his observation terms over into theoretical contexts, variously embedded. Somehow he learns to connect his observation sentences with standing sentences, sentences whose truth values do not depend on the occasion of utterance. It is only by such moves, however ill understood, that anyone masters the non-observational part of his mother tongue. He can learn the observational part in firm and well-understood ways, and then he must build out somehow, imitating what he hears and linking it tenuously and conjecturally to what he knows, until by dint of trial and social correction he achieves fluent dialogue with his community. This discourse depends, for whatever empirical content it has, on its devious and tenuous connections with the observation sentences; and those are the same connections, nearly enough, through which one has achieved one's fluent part in that discourse. The channels by which, having learned observation sentences, we acquire theoretical language, are the very channels by which observation lends evidence to scientific theory. It all stands to reason; for language is man-made and the locutions of scientific theory have no meaning but what they acquired by our learning to use them.

We see, then, a strategy for investigating the relation of evidential support, between observation and scientific theory. We can adopt a genetic approach, studying how theoretical language is learned. For the evidential relation is virtually enacted, it would seem, in the learning. This genetic strategy is attractive because the learning of language goes on in the world and is open to scientific study. It is a strategy for the scientific study of scientific method and evidence. We have here a good reason to regard the theory of language as vital to the theory of knowledge.

When we try to understand the relation between scientific theory and the observation sentences, we are brought up short by the break between occasion sentences and standing sentences; for observation sentences are of the one kind while theoretical sentences are of the other. The scientific system cannot digest occasion sentences; their substance must first be converted into standing sentences. The observation sentence 'Rain' or 'It is raining' will not do; we must put the information into a standing sentence: 'Rain at Heathrow 1600 G.M.T. 23 February 1974.' This report is ready for filing in the archives of science. It still reports an observation, but it is a standing report rather than an occasion sentence. How do we get from the passing observation of rain to the standing report?

This can be explained by a cluster of observations and observation sentences, having to do with other matters besides the rain. Thus take the term 'Heathrow'. Proper names of persons, buildings, and localities are best treated as observation terms, on a par with 'red' and 'rain'. All such terms can be learned by ostension, repeated sufficiently to suggest the intended scope and limits of application. 'Here is Heathrow,' then, is an observation sentence on a par with 'It is raining'; and their conjunction, 'Raining at Heathrow,' is an observation sentence as well. It is an occasion sentence still, of course, and not a standing report of observation. But now the two further needed ingredients, hour and date, can be added as pointer readings: 'The clock reads 1600' and 'The calendar reads 23 February 1974' are further observation sentences. Taking the conjunction of all four, we still have an observation sentence: 'Rain at Heathrow with clock at 1600 and calendar at 23 February 1974.' But it is an observation sentence with this curious trait: it gives lasting information, dependent no longer on the vicissitudes of tense or of indicator words like 'here' and 'now'. It is suitable for filing.

True, the clock and calendar may have been wrong. As an observation sentence our report must be viewed as stating the temporal readings and not the temporal facts. The question of the temporal facts belongs to scientific theory, somewhat above the observational level. Theoretical repercussions of this and other observations could eventually even prompt a modest scientific hypothesis to the effect that the clock or the calendar had been wrong.

I think this example serves pretty well as a paradigm case, to show how we can get from the occasion sentences of observation to the standing reports of observation that are needed for scientific theory. But this connection is by no means the only connection between observation sentences and standing sentences. Thus consider the universal categorical, 'A dog is an animal.' This is a standing sentence, but it is not, like the example of rain at Heathrow, a standing report of observation. Let us resume our genetic strategy: how might a child have mastered such a universal categorical?

I shall venture one hypothesis, hoping that it may be improved upon. The child has learned to assent to the observation term 'a dog' when it is queried in the conspicuous presence of dogs, and he has learned to assent to 'an animal' likewise when it is queried in the conspicuous presence of dogs (though not only dogs). Because of his close association of the word 'dog' with dogs, the mere sound of the word 'dog' disposes him to respond to the subsequent query 'an animal' as he would have done if a dog had been there; so he assents when he hears 'a dog' followed by the query, 'an animal?'. Being rewarded for so doing, he ever after assents to the query 'A dog is an animal?' In the same way he learns a few other examples of the universal categorical. Next he rises to a mastery of the universal categorical construction 'An S is a P' in general: he learns to apply it to new cases on his own. This important step of abstraction can perhaps be explained in parallel fashion to the early learning of observation sentences, namely, by simple induction along similarity lines; but the similarity now is a language-dependent similarity.

Much the same account can be offered for the learning of the seemingly simpler construction, mere predication: 'Fido is a dog,' 'Sugar is sweet.'

The child has now made creditable progress from observation sentences towards theoretical language, by mastering predication and the universal categorical construction. Another important step will be mastery of the relative clause; and I think I can give a convincing hypothesis of how this comes about. What is conspicuous about the relative clause is its role in predication. Thus take a relative clause, 'something that chases its tail', and predicate it of Dinah: 'Dinah is something that chases its tail.' This is equivalent to the simple sentence 'Dinah chases its tail' (or 'her tail'). When we predicate the relative clause, the effect is the same as substituting the subject of the predication for the pronoun of the relative clause. Now my suggestion regarding the learning of the relative clause is that the child learns this substitution transformation. He discovers that the adult is prepared to assent to a predication of a relative clause in just the circumstances where he is prepared to assent to the simpler sentence obtained by the substitution.

This explains how the child could learn relative clauses in one standard position: predicative position. He learns how to eliminate them, in that position, by the substitution transformation—and how to introduce them into that position by the converse transformation, superstition. But then, having learned this much, he is struck by an analogy between relative clauses and ordinary simple predicates or general terms; for these also appear in predicative position. So, pursuing the analogy, he presses relative clauses into other positions where general terms have been appearing—notably into the universal categorical construction. Or, if the child does not press this analogy on his own, he is at any rate well prepared to grasp adult usage and follow it in the light of the analogy. In this way the relative clause gets into the universal categorical construction, from which it cannot be eliminated by the substitution transformation. It is there to stay.

We can easily imagine how the child might learn the truth functions—negation, conjunction, alternation. Take conjunction: the child notices, by degrees, that the adult affirms 'p and q' in only those circumstances where he is disposed, if queried, to assent to 'p' and also to 'q'.

We have now seen, in outline and crude conjecture, how one might start at the observational edge of language and work one's way into the discursive interior where scientific theory can begin to be expressed. Predication is at hand, and the universal categorical, the relative clause, and the truth functions. Once this stage is reached, it is easy to see that the whole strength of logical quantification is available. I shall not pause over the details of this, except to remark that the pronouns of relative clauses take on the role of the bound variable of quantification. By further conjectures in the same spirit, some of them more convincing and some less, we can outline the learner's further progress, to where he is bandying abstract terms and quantifying over properties, numbers, functions, and hypothetical physical particles and forces. This progress is not a continuous derivation, which, followed backward, would enable us to reduce scientific theory to sheer observation. It is a progress rather by short leaps of analogy. One such was the pressing of relative clauses into universal categoricals, where they cease to be eliminable. There are further such psychological speculations that I could report, but time does not allow.

Such speculations would gain, certainly, from experimental investigation of the child's actual learning of language. Experimental findings already available in the literature could perhaps be used to sustain or correct these conjectures at points, and further empirical investigations could be devised. But a speculative approach of the present sort seems required to begin with, in order to isolate just the factual questions that bear on our purposes. For our objective here is still philosophical—a better understanding of the relations between evidence and scientific theory. Moreover, the way to this objective requires consideration of linguistics and logic along with psychology. This is why the speculative phase has to precede, for the most part, the formulation of relevant questions to be posed to the experimental psychologist.

In any event the present speculations, however inaccurate, are presumably true to the general nature of language acquisition. And already they help us to understand how the logical links are forged that connect theoretical sentences with the reports of observation. We learn the grammatical construction 'p and q' by learning, among other things, to assent to the compound only in circumstances where we are disposed to assent to each component. Thus it is that the logical law of inference which leads from 'p and q' to 'p' is built into our habits by the very learning of 'and'. Similarly for the other laws of conjunction, and correspondingly for the laws of alternation and other truth functions. Correspondingly, again, for laws of quantification. The law of inference that leads from '$(x)Fx$' to 'Fa' should be traceable back, through the derivation of quantification that I have passed over, until it is found finally to hinge upon the substitution transformation by which we learn to use the relative clause. Thus, in general, the acquisition of our basic logical habits is to be accounted for in our acquisition of grammatical constructions.

Related remarks hold true of inferential habits that exceed pure logic. We learn when to assent to 'dog', and to 'animal', only by becoming disposed to assent to 'animal' in all circumstances where we will assent to 'dog'. Connections more accidental and casual in aspect can also come about through the learning of words; thus a child may have begun to learn the term 'good' in application to chocolate.

I characterized science as a linguistic structure that is keyed to observation here and there. I said also that it is an instrument for predicting observations on the basis of earlier observations. It is keyed to observations, earlier and later, forming a labyrinthine connection between them; and it is through this labyrinth that the prediction takes place. A powerful improvement, this, over simple induction from past observations to future ones; powerful and costly. I have now sketched the nature of the connection between the observations and the labyrinthine interior of scientific theory. I have sketched it in terms of the learning of language. This seemed reasonable, since the scientist himself can make no sense of the language of scientific theory beyond what goes into his learning of it. The paths of language learning, which lead from observation sentences to theoretical sentences, are the only connection there is between observation and theory. This has been a sketch, but a fuller understanding may be sought along the same line: by a more painstaking investigation of how we learn theoretical language.

One important point that already stands forth, regarding the relation of theory to observation, is the vast freedom that the form of the theory must enjoy, relative even to all possible observation. Theory is empirically under-determined. Surely even if we had an observational oracle, capable of assigning a truth value to every standing observational report expressible in our language, still this would not suffice to adjudicate between a host of possible physical theories, each of them completely in accord with the oracle. This seems clear in view of the tenuousness of the connections that we have noted between observation sentences and theoretical ones. At the level of observation sentences, even the general form of the eventual theoretical language remained indeterminate, to say nothing of the ontology. The observation sentences were associated, as wholes, with the stimulatory situations that warranted assent to them; but there was in this no hint of what aspects of the stimulatory situations to single out somehow as objects, if indeed any. The question of ontology simply makes no sense until we get to something recognizable as quantification, or perhaps as a relative clause, with pronouns as potential variables. At the level of observation sentences there was no foreseeing even that the superimposed theoretical language would contain anything recognizable as quantification or relative clauses. The steps by which the child was seen to progress from observational language to relative clauses and categoricals and quantification had the arbitrary character of historical accident and cultural heritage; there was no hint of inevitability.

It was a tremendous achievement, on the part of our long-term culture and our latter-day scientists, to develop a theory that leads from observation to predicted observation as successfully as ours. It is a near miracle. If our theory were in full conformity with the observational oracle that we just now imagined, which surely it is not, that would be yet a nearer miracle. But if, even granted that nearer miracle, our theory were not still just one of many equally perfect possible theories to the same observational effect, that would be too miraculous to make sense.

But it must be said that the issue of under-determination proves slippery when we try to grasp it more firmly. If two theories conform to the same totality of possible observations, in what sense are they two? Perhaps they are both stated in English, and they are alike, word for word, except that one of them calls molecules electrons and electrons molecules. Literally the two theories are in contradiction, saying incompatible things about so-called molecules. But of course we would not want to count this case; we would call it terminological. Or again, following Poincaré, suppose the two theories are alike except that one of them assumes an infinite space while the other has a finite space in which bodies shrink in proportion to their distance from centre. Even here we want to say that the difference is rather terminological than real; and our reason is that we see how to bring the theories into agreement by translation: by reconstruing the English of one of the theories.

At this point it may be protested that after all there can never be two complete theories agreeing on the total output of the observational oracle. It may be protested that since such theories would be empirically equivalent, would have the same empirical meaning, their difference is purely verbal. For surely there is no meaning but empirical meaning, and theories with the same meaning must be seen as translations one of the other. This argument simply rules out, by definition, the doctrine that physical theory is under-determined by all possible observation.

The best reaction at this point is to back away from terminology and sort things out on their merits. Where the significant difference comes is perhaps where we no longer see how to state rules of translation that would bring the two empirically equivalent theories together. Terminology aside, what wants recognizing is that a physical theory of radically different form from ours, with nothing even recognizably similar to our quantification or objective reference, might still be empirically equivalent to ours, in the sense of predicting the same episodes of sensory bombardment on the strength of the same past episodes. Once this is recognized, the scientific achievement of our culture becomes in a way more impressive than ever. For, in the midst of all this formless freedom for variation, our science has developed in such a way as to maintain always a manageably narrow spectrum of visible alternatives among which to choose when need arises to revise a theory. It is this narrowing of sights, or tunnel vision, that has made for the continuity of science, through the vicissitudes of refutation and correction. And it is this also that has fostered the illusion of there being only one solution to the riddle of the universe.

5 *Mind and Verbal Dispositions*

W. V. QUINE

DESCARTES supposed that man is the only animal endowed with mind; the others are automata. It is held further, and more widely and on better evidence, that man is the only animal endowed with language. Now if man is unique in enjoying these two gifts, it is no coincidence. One may argue that no mindless creature could cope with so intricate a device as language. Or one may argue conversely that no appreciable mental activity is conceivable without linguistic aids.

Most thought simply *is* speech, according to the pioneer behaviourist John B. Watson: silent, repressed, incipient speech. Not all thought is that. A geometer or an engineer may think by means also of little incipient tugs of the muscles that are used in drawing curves or twirling cogwheels. Still, the muscles that play by far the major role, according to Watson's muscular theory of meditation, are the muscles used in making speeches.

Conversely, there is an age-old and persistent tendency to try to explain and analyse the physical phenomenon of speech by appealing to mind, mental activity, and mental entities: by appealing to thoughts, ideas, meanings. Language, we are told, serves to convey ideas. We learn language from our elders by learning to associate the words with the same ideas with which our elders have learned to associate them. Thus it is, we may be told, that approximate uniformity of association of words with ideas is achieved and maintained throughout the community.

Such an account would of course be extravagantly perverse. Thus consider the case where we teach the infant a word by reinforcing his random babbling on some appropriate occasion. His chance utterance bears a chance resemblance to a word appropriate to the occasion, and we reward him. The occasion must be some object or some stimulus source that we as well as the child are in a position to notice. Furthermore, we must be in a position to observe that the child is in a position to notice it. Only thus would there be any purpose in our rewarding his chance utterance. In so doing we encourage the child to repeat the word on future similar occasions. But are we causing him to associate the word with the same *idea* that we adults associate it with? Do we adults all associate it with the same idea ourselves, for that matter? And what would that mean?

The moral of this is that the fixed points are just the shared stimulus and the word; the ideas in between are as may be and may vary as they please, so long as the external stimulus in question stays paired up with the word in question for all concerned. The point is well dramatized by the familiar fantasy of complementary colour perception. Who knows but that I see things in colours opposite to those in which you see the things? For communication it is a matter of indifference.

I believe in the affinity of mind and language, but I want to keep the relation right side up. Watson's theory of thought, however inadequate, has matters right side up. A theory of mind can gain clarity and substance, I think, from a better understanding of the workings of language, whereas little understanding of the workings of language is to be hoped for in mentalistic terms.

I shall say a little about how it is that people feel drawn to a mentalistic account of language, despite the conspicuous fact that language is a social enterprise which is keyed to intersubjectively observable objects in the external world. Also I shall speculate on how we might hope to get on with a properly physicalistic account of language. First I must talk a little more about learning.

I mentioned one primitive way of learning a word: through reinforcement of random babbling. Another way, somewhat the reverse, is imitation. In the case of babbling it was the adult that witnessed what was confronting the child when the child chanced to babble the appropriate word. In the case of imitation it is the child, conversely, that witnesses what is confronting the adult when the adult volunteers the word. The child then volunteers the word when similarly confronted, and thereupon the adult proceeds to reinforce the child's behaviour just as in the case of babbling. The imitation method is more sophisticated than the babbling method. It can still be explained, indirectly, in terms of stimulus and reinforced response; but I won't pause over it.

What we do need to notice is that all language learning at this primitive level is directed only to the learning of what may be called observation terms, or, more properly, observation sentences. The child learns to assent to the query 'red?' in the conspicuous presence of red things. Also he masters the trick of getting the object by uttering the word; 'red' is a poor example here, but 'ball' and 'milk' and 'Mama' are clear cases. Also he masters the word in a passive way, responding in some distinctive fashion on hearing it. He may respond by turning to face the object, or by fetching it.

Now the observation term, or observation sentence, is a ground on which John the rational animal and Fido the automaton can meet and to some degree communicate. The dog learns observation sentences in his passive way. He learns to respond to them by salivating, by running to the kitchen, by turning to face the object, or by fetching it.

Already at this lowly level of observation sentences the small child differs from the dog, it may seem, in that he learns the sentences also actively: he utters them. This still is not a clear contrast. Dogs learn to ask for things, in their inarticulate way. Let us not arrogate to rationality what may be merely superior agility of lips and tongue and larynx. Premack and his chimpanzee have circumvented these muscular obstacles by resorting to plastic symbols, which they push around on a board. Premack succeeds in teaching his chimpanzee to volunteer observation sentences appropriately and to play a passable game of query and assent.

A contrast that has long been remarked, between human language and animal signals, is the combinatorial productivity of language: man's ability to compose new and unprecedented sentences from old materials, and to respond appropriately to such new creations. But Premack reports that his chimpanzee even passes this test, within modest limits. It would thus appear that combinatorial productivity in language affords no sharp line between man and beast. Man may plume himself on having been the first to develop a combinatorially productive language, but the ability to learn it may be more widespread.

Combinatorial productivity, however, is not the only trait that has seemed to distinguish mind-governed discourse from the performance of trained animals. A major factor is the unpredictable spontaneity of speech. Animal drives are still at work behind the torrent of human speech, but they are seldom clearly to be traced. Even if in our verbal output we differ from Premack's chimpanzee only in degree and not in kind, still it is this overwhelming difference of degree that invites the mentalistic accounts of verbal behaviour. The torrent of words is seen as a manifestation of the speaker's inner life beyond animal drives. Nowadays one is apt to resort thus to a mentalistic semantics not so much because one sees an ontological gulf between man and the apes, as because one despairs of adhering to the standards of natural science in coping with the complexities of intelligent discourse.

The central notion in mentalistic semantics is an unanalysed notion of meaning. It figures mainly in two contexts: where we speak of knowing the meaning of an expression, and where we speak of sameness of meaning. We say we know the meaning of an expression when we are able to produce a clearer or more familiar expression having the same meaning. We ask the meaning of an expression when what we want is a clearer or more familiar expression having the same meaning.

I said to my small son, 'Eighty-two. You know what I mean?' He said, 'No.' Then I said to my small daughter, 'Ottantadue. You know what I mean?' She said, 'Yes. Eighty-two.' I said, 'See, Margaret understands Italian better than Douglas understands English.'

Our ways of talking of meaning are thus misleading. To understand an expression is, one would say, to know the meaning; and to know the meaning is, one would say, to be able to give the meaning. Yet Douglas could rightly claim to *understand* the expression 'eighty-two', despite answering 'No' to 'You know what I mean?' He answered 'No' because he was unable to *give* the meaning; and he was unable to give the meaning because what we call giving the meaning consists really in the asymmetrical operation of producing an equivalent expression that is clearer. Margaret was ready with a clearer equivalent of 'ottantadue', but Douglas was at a loss for a *still* clearer equivalent of 'eighty-two'. In another context he might have ventured, 'Yes, you mean the temperature is eighty-two.'

People persist in talking thus of knowing the meaning, and of giving the meaning, and of sameness of meaning, where they could omit mention of meaning and merely talk of understanding an expression, or talk of the equivalence of expressions and the paraphrasing of expressions. They do so because the notion of meaning is felt somehow to *explain* the understanding and equivalence of expressions. We understand expressions by knowing or grasping their meanings; and one expression serves as a translation or paraphrase of another because they mean the same. It is of course spurious explanation, mentalistic explanation at its worst. The paradoxical little confusion between understanding 'eighty-two' and knowing or giving its meaning is always symptomatic of awkward concept-building; but where the real threat lies, in talking of meaning, is in the illusion of explanation.

In all we may distinguish three levels of purported explanation, three degrees of depth: the mental, the behavioural, and the physiological. The mental is the most superficial of these, scarcely deserving the name of explanation. The physiological is the deepest and most ambitious, and it is the place for causal explanations. The behavioural level, in between, is what we must settle for in our descriptions of language, in our formulations of language rules, and in our explications of semantical terms. It is here, if anywhere, that we must give our account of the understanding of an expression, and our account of the equivalence that holds between an expression and its translation or paraphrase. These things need to be explained, if at all, in behavioural terms: in terms of dispositions to overt gross behaviour.

Take understanding. Part of the understanding of a word consists in the ability to use it properly in all manner of admissible contexts. Part consists in reacting properly to all such uses. So there is a good deal here to sort out and organize. We must divide and define. To begin with we can set aside the complication of the myriad sentential contexts of a word, by beginning rather with sentences as wholes: with complete little isolated speeches, consisting perhaps of a single word and perhaps of more.

Bewildering variety confronts us even so. One and the same little sentence may be uttered for various purposes: to warn, to remind, to obtain possession, to gain confirmation, to gain admiration, or to give pleasure by pointing something out. The occasions for uttering one and the same sentence are so various that we can seldom predict when a sentence will be uttered or which one it will be. An unpromising setting, this, in which to explore and exploit verbal dispositions. Somehow we must further divide; we must find some significant central strand to extract from the tangle.

Truth will do nicely. Some sentences, of course, do not have truth values: thus questions and imperatives. Those that do may still be uttered for a variety of reasons unconnected with instruction; I just now enumerated some. But, among these sentences, truth is a great

leveller, enabling us to postpone consideration of all those trouble-
some excrescences. Here, then, is an adjusted standard of understanding: a man understands a sentence in so far as he knows its truth
conditions. This kind of understanding stops short of humour, irony,
innuendo, and other literary values, but it goes a long way. In particular it is all we can ask of an understanding of the language of
science.

We are interested not only in explaining what it is for someone else
to understand a sentence, but also in setting a standard for ourselves,
as when we try to penetrate a new language and to understand its
sentences, or try to teach the language. Our standard, still, is this:
give the truth conditions. Hence Davidson's plan for a semantics in
the style of Tarski's truth definition.

But when I define the understanding of a sentence as knowledge of
its truth conditions I am certainly not offering a definition to rest
with; my term 'knowledge' is as poor a resting-point as the term
'understanding' itself.

We were supposed to be getting things down to terms of dispositions to behaviour. In what behavioural disposition then does a man's
knowledge of the truth conditions of the sentence 'This is red' consist? Not, certainly, in a disposition to affirm the sentence on every
occasion of observing a red object, and to deny it on all other occasions; it is the disposition to assent or dissent when asked in the
presence or absence of red. Query and assent, query and dissent—
here is the solvent that reduces understanding to verbal disposition.
Without this device there would be no hope of handing language
down the generations, nor any hope of breaking into newly discovered languages. It is primarily by querying sentences for assent
and dissent that we tap the reservoirs of verbal disposition.

This approach applies primarily to terms, or occasion sentences,
rather than to standing sentences. For the disposition to assent to or
dissent from the sentence 'This is red' is marked by a correlation between assent and the presence of red, and between dissent and the
absence of red, on occasions where the sentence is queried. A standing sentence, whose truth value remains fixed over long periods,
offers no significant correlation of the kind. Where the method of
queried assent and dissent is at its best, indeed, is in application to
occasion sentences of the special sort that I have called observation
sentences; for the occasions that make the sentence true are going to
have to be intersubjectively recognizable if we are to be able to *tell*

whether the speaker has the disposition in question. Even in these cases, of course, we remain at the mercy of the speaker's veracity: we assume when querying him that his assents and dissents are sincere. Happily we live in a moral climate where this assumption generally holds up; language could not flourish otherwise.

Standing sentences can be queried too, but the stimulating situation at the time of querying them will usually have no bearing on the verdict; and for this reason we cannot identify the understanding of a standing sentence, even approximately, with a disposition to assent or dissent when queried on particular occasions. I do not know how, in general, in terms of behavioural dispositions, to approximate to the notion of understanding at all, when the sentences understood are standing sentences. Perhaps it cannot be done, taking standing sentences one by one.

Once in a while we get a hint of a specifically relevant disposition, still, when we find someone reversing his verdict on a standing sentence in the face of some observation. But with all conceivable luck we cannot hope to correlate standing sentences generally with observations, because the sentences one by one simply do not have their own separable empirical implications. A multiplicity of standing sentences will interlock, rather, as a theory; and an observation in conflict with that theory may be accommodated by revoking one or other of the sentences—no one sentence in particular.

One sees how a semanticist might despair and seek shelter in the jungle of mentalistic semantics. But there are other courses. Perhaps the very notion of understanding, as applied to single standing sentences, simply cannot be explicated in terms of behavioural dispositions. Perhaps therefore it is simply an untenable notion, notwithstanding our intuitive predilections. It stands to reason that a proper semantical analysis of standing sentences, in terms of behavioural dispositions, will be primarily occupied with the interrelations of sentences rather than with standing sentences one by one.

I mentioned two central semantical notions which, in mentalistic semantics, are obscured by talk of meaning. One was the notion of understanding an expression, and the other was the relation of equivalence between an expression and its paraphrase. Afterwards I considered what might be done about understanding. Now what about the other notion, the equivalence relation? Much of what I have said about understanding applies in parallel fashion to equivalence. Here, as there, we can conveniently organize our work by looking first to sentences as wholes, seeking an equivalence concept for them. Here, as there, we can usefully narrow our problem by focusing on truth conditions and so exploiting a method of query and assent. And here, of course, as there, the sentences that prove reasonably amenable are the occasion sentences, especially the observation sentences. What relates such a sentence to its equivalent is simply a coinciding of dispositions: we are disposed to assent to both sentences in the same circumstances.

Moreover, in a behavioural account of equivalence, just as in a behavioural account of understanding, we encounter difficulty when we move to standing sentences. Since a man is apt to assent to a standing sentence, if asked, in all sorts of circumstances or in none, the coinciding of dispositions to assent to two standing sentences gives no basis for equating them.

I am persuaded, indeed, that a satisfactory equivalence concept is impossible for standing sentences. My view of this matter can be conveyed most clearly if we consider translation between two languages. I am persuaded that alternative manuals of translation can exist, incompatible with each other, and both of them conforming fully to the dispositions to behaviour on the part of the speakers of the two languages. The two manuals would agree on observation sentences but conflict in some of the standing sentences. Each manual, being a manual of translation, purports to specify the equivalence relation between sentences and their translations, and neither manual is right to the exclusion of the other.

This indeterminacy of translation is unsuspected in mentalistic semantics, because of the facile talk of meaning. Sentences have meanings, and a translation is right if it has the same meaning. Mentalistic semantics requires that one of two conflicting manuals of translation be wrong, though it conforms to every speaker's dispositions. Mentalistic semantics thus sets a false goal, which, even though vague and ill defined, tends to obstruct other lines of thought.

Of course, translation must go on. Indeterminacy means that there is more than one way; we can still proceed to develop one of them, as good as any. And, in a more theoretical mood, we must still consider what counts as evidence for *an* acceptable translation relation, even if the relation is not unique. The evidence will be behavioural still, of course, even though the relation is no simple coinciding of behavioural dispositions, as it was in the case of the equivalence of observation sentences. We have to examine relations of interdependence between verbal dispositions: systematic interdependences between dispositions to assent to standing sentences and dispositions to assent in certain circumstances to observation sentences. Here again, in the problem of equivalence as in the problem of understanding, it would seem that genetic semantics offers a likely approach. But we must expect no simple picture, no easy answers. For it is a question again of the relations of standing sentences to observation sentences, and hence nothing less than the relation of scientific theory to scientific evidence.

Let us then recognize that the semantical study of language is worth pursuing with all the scruples of the natural scientist. We must study language as a system of dispositions to verbal behaviour, and not just surface listlessly to the Sargasso Sea of mentalism.

It has been objected that when I talk of query and assent I am not really escaping mentalism after all, because assent itself has a mental component. It is objected that assent is no mere mindless parroting of an arbitrary syllable; utterance of the syllable counts as assent only if there is the appropriate mental act behind it. Very well, let us adopt the term *surface assent* for the utterance or gesture itself. My behavioural approach does indeed permit me, then, only to appeal to surface assent; assent as I talk of it must be understood as surface assent. This behavioural notion has its powers, however, and must not be underrated. For the syllable or gesture of assent in a community is not identified at random, after all; it is itself singled out, in turn, by behavioural criteria. One partial criterion of what to count as a sign of assent is that a speaker is disposed to produce that sign whenever a sentence is queried in circumstances in which he would be disposed to volunteer the sentence himself. Even surface assent, thus, is not just the parroting of any arbitrary syllable. Granted, some cases of surface assent are insincere, but happily they are rare enough, as I have already remarked, to permit the field linguist still to find laws and translations on the strength of statistical trends.

I have been inveighing against mentalistic semantics and urging in its place the study of dispositions to behaviour. This move could be represented alternatively and more picturesquely as a matter not so much of substitution as of identification: let us *construe* mind as a system of disposition to behaviour. This version somewhat recalls Gilbert Ryle and Wilfrid Sellars, who have urged a generally dispositional philosophy of mind. Some small further encouragement for it may be seen in the fact that even our most ordinary and characteristic mentalistic idioms already take almost the form of attributions of verbal dispositions. These are the idioms of propositional attitude: '*x* believes that *p*', '*x* wishes that *p*', '*x* expects that *p*', and so on. They all follow the broad pattern of indirect quotation, '*x* says that *p*', as if to attribute to *x* the disposition to utter the sentence '*p*' in some mood. Thus *x* believes that *p* if, approximately, he will affirm *p*; he wishes or regrets that *p* if, approximately, he will exclaim 'Oh that *p*!' or 'Alas, *p*!'

I am offering no proper analysis of the propositional attitudes. People do not volunteer all their beliefs in affirmations. A better criterion of belief is the disposition to assent if asked; and this still leaves no room for questioning sincerity. Also there is the problem of allowable latitude of translation or paraphrase, when the '*p*' clause in '*x* believes that *p*' contains words alien to *x*'s actual vocabulary. This question of allowable latitude of course arises acutely in indirect discourse itself, '*x* said that *p*', and it plagues all the idioms of propositional attitude. And finally there are quandaries over the referential opacity of the idioms of propositional attitude: quandaries having to do with the substitutivity of identity, and with quantifying into opaque contexts. All in all, the propositional attitudes are in a bad way. These are the idioms most stubbornly at variance with scientific patterns. Consequently I find it particularly striking that these, of all idioms, already describe mental states in a way that hints at dispositions to verbal behaviour. A philosophy of mind as verbal disposition is after all not so very alien to deep-rooted popular attitudes.

I spoke of three levels of purported explanation: the mental, the behavioural, and the physiological. We have just now been contemplating the second, the behavioural. Now the relation of this level to the third and deepest, the physiological, begins to be evident when we examine the notion of a *disposition* to behaviour and consider what we mean by a disposition.

A disposition is in my view simply a physical trait, a configuration or mechanism. It can be a disjunctive physical trait, since like effects can come of unlike mechanisms. What makes it a disposition is no significant character of its own, but only the style in which we happen to specify it. Thus take the classical example, solubility in water. This is a physical trait that can be specified, with varying degrees of thoroughness, in various ways. It can be described quite fully, I gather, in terms of the relative positions of small particles. It can also be described, less fully, by citing a simple test: put an object in water and see if it dissolves. Instructions for this convenient test are compactly encoded, as it happens, in the adjective 'soluble' itself, with its verb stem 'solu-' and its dispositional ending '-ble'. The adjective 'soluble' is a disposition word, and this is an important classification of words; but the physical traits themselves do not divide into dispositions and others, any more significantly than mankind divides into passers-by and others. The term 'disposition' has its significant application rather as a preface, each time, to an actual singling out of some physical trait; thus we may significantly specify some physical trait as the disposition to behave thus and so in such-and-such circumstances. It is this that is accomplished also, and more laconically, by dispositional adjectives such as 'soluble', 'fragile', 'docile', 'portable'. The dispositional way of specifying physical traits is as frequent and as useful as it is because we are so often not prepared, as we now happen to be in the case of solubility, to specify the intended physical trait in other than the dispositional style.

The dispositional way of specifying physical states and traits is indeed pretty generally *the* way of specifying them, except at high levels of scientific theory. The explicit dispositional idiom does not always appear, either as the word 'disposition' or as a suffix '-ble' or '-ile'; commonly the dispositional force is only implicit. Hardness, for instance, is the disposition to resist if pressed, or to scratch. Redness, said of a body, is the disposition to blush in white light. Hardness and redness come finally, like solubility, to be explained in terms of minute structure, but our first access to these physical traits is dispositional. In fact the same may be said of the very notion of body itself; for a body comes to be known, as Kant remarked, by its disposition to present a repcatable sequence of views as we walk around it or revisit it. True to form, even this disposition qualifies as a physical mechanism: *body*. Like the other physical mechanisms, this one also comes in the fulness of time to be explained in terms of small particles.

John Stuart Mill's characterization of a body as 'a permanent possibility of sensation' was meant in an idealistic spirit, as a reduction of matter to sensory disposition. Thanks to symmetry, however, the identity admits also of a materialistic inversion: corporeality, like solubility, is an objective physical arrangement of particles, but known first in dispositional terms.

Dispositions to behaviour, then, are physiological states or traits or mechanisms. In citing them dispositionally we are singling them out by behavioural symptoms, behavioural tests. Usually we are in no position to detail them in physiological terms, but in this there is no anomaly; we also commonly specify ailments *per accidens*, citing gross signs and symptoms and knowing no physiological details.

We now see the relation of the second level of explanation, the behavioural, to the third and deepest level, the physiological. At the second level we treat of dispositions to behaviour, and these dispositions are indeed physiological states, but we identify them only by their behavioural manifestations. The deepest explanation, the physiological, would analyse these dispositions in explicit terms of nerve impulses and other anatomically and chemically identified organic processes.

Our three levels thus are levels of reduction: mind consists in dispositions to behaviour, and these are physiological states. We recall that John B. Watson did not claim that quite *all* thought was incipient speech; it was all incipient twitching of muscles, and *mostly* of speech muscles. Just so, I would not identify mind quite wholly with verbal disposition; with Ryle and Sellars I would identify it with behavioural disposition, and *mostly* verbal. And then, having construed behavioural dispositions in turn as physiological states, I end up with the so-called identity theory of mind: mental states are states of the body.

However, a word of caution is in order regarding the so-called identity theory. How does it differ from a repudiation theory? Let us think for a moment about an analogous question elsewhere, concerning the definitions of natural number in set theory. We may say that numbers are defined as sets in Frege's way, or in Zermelo's way, or in von Neumann's way, these ways all being good but incompatible. Or we may say that numbers may be repudiated, dispensed with; that we can get along with just sets instead, in any of various ways— Frege's way, Zermelo's way, von Neumann's way. This repudiation version has the advantage that we no longer seem called upon to adjudicate between three identifications of the natural numbers, the three being incompatible and yet all somehow correct.

Correspondingly, instead of saying that mental states are identical with physiological ones, we could repudiate them; we could claim that they can be dispensed with, in all our theorizing, in favour of physiological states, these being specified usually not in actual physiological terms but in the idiom of behavioural dispositions. This repudiation version has a certain advantage, though a different one from what we noted in the case of number. Its advantage here is that it discourages a possible abuse of the identity theory. For, product though the identity theory is of hard-headed materialism, we must beware of its sedative use to relieve intellectual discomfort. We can imagine someone appealing to the identity theory to excuse his own free and uncritical recourse to mentalistic semantics. We can imagine him pleading that it is after all just a matter of physiology, even if no one knows quite how. This would be a sad irony indeed, and the repudiation theory has the virtue, over the identity theory, of precluding it.

Until we can aspire to actual physiological explanation of linguistic activity in physiological terms, the level at which to work is the middle one; that of dispositions to overt behaviour. Its virtue is not that it affords causal explanations but that it is less likely than the mentalistic level to engender an illusion of being more explanatory than it is. The easy familiarity of mentalistic talk is not to be trusted.

Still, among the dispositions to behaviour, some are more explanatory than others. The ones that we should favour, in explanations, are the ones whose physiological mechanisms seem likeliest to be detected in the foreseeable future. To cite a behavioural disposition is to posit an unexplained neural mechanism, and such posits should be made in the hope of their submitting some day to a physical explanation.

6 *What is a Theory of Meaning?*[1]

M. A. E. DUMMETT

ACCORDING to one well-known view, the best method of formulating the philosophical problems surrounding the concept of meaning and related notions is by asking what form that should be taken by what is called 'a theory of meaning' for any one entire language; that is, a detailed specification of the meanings of all the words and sentence-forming operations of the language, yielding a specification of the meaning of every expression and sentence of the language. It is not that the construction of a theory of meaning, in this sense, for any one language is viewed as a practical project; but it is thought that, when once we can enunciate the general principles in accordance with which such a construction could be carried out, we shall have arrived at a solution of the problems concerning meaning by which philosophers are perplexed.

I share the belief that this is the most fruitful approach to the problems within this area of philosophy, although I should not feel capable of giving a demonstration that this was so to someone who denied it: but we can see some reasons for it if we contrast certain other cases. So far as I know, no one has ever suggested a parallel approach to the problems of epistemology: no one has proposed that the right way to go about tackling the philosophical problems relating to the concept of knowledge would be by considering how one might construct a theory of knowledge in the sense of a detailed specification of everything that any one individual, or community, can be said to know. The reason is, I think, that our grasp on the concept of knowledge is rather more secure than our grasp on the concept of meaning. We are in doubt about what ought to count as knowledge; we are even more in doubt about how to formulate the principles we tacitly apply for deciding whether or not something is

[1] This is the first part of a two-part answer to this question. The second is to appear in *Essays in Semantics*, edited by Gareth Evans and John McDowell, Clarendon Press, Oxford.

to count as knowledge; we also have some uncertainty about the semantic analysis of a sentence attributing knowledge of something to somebody: but at least we are quite certain *which* are the sentences whose logical form and whose truth conditions we are seeking to analyse. By contrast, while most of us, myself included, would agree that the concept of meaning is a fundamental and indispensable one, we are unclear even about the surface structure of statements involving that concept. What kind of sentence, of natural language, should be taken as the characteristic form for an attribution of a particular meaning to some given word or expression? Not only do we not know the answer to this: we do not even know whether it is the right question to ask. Perhaps it is impossible, in general, to *state* the meaning of an expression: perhaps we ought, rather, to inquire by what linguistic means, or possibly even non-linguistic means, it is possible to *convey* the meaning of an expression, otherwise than by explicitly stating it. Or perhaps even that is wrong: perhaps the question should be, not how we express that a particular expression has a certain meaning, but how we should analyse sentences which involve the concept of meaning in some different way. It is precisely because, in this area of philosophy, we know even less what it is that we are talking about than we do in other areas, that the proposal to approach our problems by considering how we might attempt to specify the meanings of the expressions of an entire language does not appear the waste of time that an analogous proposal would seem to be within epistemology.

As is well known, some, pre-eminently Quine, have preferred to circumvent this difficulty by investigating the principles underlying the construction not of a theory of meaning for a language, but of a translation manual from it into some known language. The advantage is that we know exactly what form a translation manual has to take, namely an effective set of rules for mapping sentences of the translated language into sentences of the language into which the translation is being made: we can therefore concentrate entirely upon the questions how we are to arrive at a system of translation as embodied in such a manual, and what conditions must be satisfied for such a system to be acceptable. The disadvantage is that, while the interest of such an inquiry must lie in the light it throws on the concept of meaning, we are unable to be certain what consequences the results of the inquiry into translation do have for the notion of meaning, just because they are stated without direct appeal to that notion.

To grasp the meaning of an expression is to understand its role in the language: a complete theory of meaning for a language is, therefore, a complete theory of how the language functions as a language. Our interest in meaning, as a general concept, is, thus, an interest in how language works; a direct description of the way a language works— of all that someone has to learn to do when he learns the language— would, accordingly, resolve our perplexities in a way in which an indirect account, by means of a translation, cannot. It will quite rightly be said that the interest in the inquiry into translation attaches, not to the translation itself, but to the criteria proposed for judging the acceptability of a scheme of translation, and that these must relate to what can be observed of the working of the language to be translated. Indeed, it might plausibly be maintained that nothing short of a complete theory of meaning for the language—a complete account of the way it works—could be an adequate basis for judging the correctness of a proposed scheme of translation. I shall not attempt to adjudicate the soundness of this claim. If it is sound, then the apparent advantage of the approach via translation, rather than by asking outright what form a theory of meaning for the language should take, is wholly illusory. If it is unsound—and certainly the actual procedure of the principal practitioner of the approach via translation suggests that he takes it as unsound—then it follows that there is no immediate inference from results concerning translation to conclusions concerning meaning.

I have said that it is the job of a theory of meaning for a language to give an account of how that language works, that is, of how its speakers communicate by means of it: here 'communicate' has no more precise signification than 'do whatever may be done by the utterance of one or more sentences of the language'. And here I will repeat what I have maintained elsewhere, that a theory of meaning is a theory of understanding; that is, what a theory of meaning has to give an account of is what it is that someone knows when he knows the language, that is, when he knows the meanings of the expressions and sentences of the language. One question about the form which a theory of meaning should take is whether it should issue in direct ascriptions of meaning, that is, in propositions of the form 'The meaning of the word/sentence X is . . .' or of the form 'The word/ sentence X means . . .' If the answer to this question is affirmative, then it may seem that such a theory of meaning will have no need to advert explicitly to the notion of knowledge: if the theory allows us to say that the meaning of a given word or sentence is something or other, say Q, then, presumably, we shall likewise want to say that someone knows the meaning of that word or sentence if he knows that Q is what that word or sentence means. We shall later see reason to doubt this; but for the present let us suspend judgement. If the theory of meaning allows us to derive such direct ascriptions of meaning, and if these direct ascriptions are such as to lead in this simple way to a characterization of what it is to know the meaning of each word or sentence in the language, then, indeed, my claim that a theory of meaning must be a theory of understanding is not intended in so strong a sense as to rule out such a theory, merely on the ground that it did not itself employ the notion of knowledge: it would be proper to accept such a theory as being a theory of understanding. If, on the other hand, although the theory of meaning allows the derivation of direct ascriptions of meaning, these ascriptions are so framed as not to permit an immediate characterization of what it is that a person knows when he knows the meaning of a given word or sentence, then, by hypothesis, the theory is inadequate to account for one extremely important type of context in which we are disposed to use the word 'meaning'. If, however, the theory of meaning does not issue in such direct ascriptions of meaning at all; and if, further, it does not contain within itself any overt account of what someone has to know in order to know or grasp the meaning of each expression of the language, but merely provides an explanation of other contexts in which we use the word 'meaning', such as 'X means the same as Y' or 'X has a meaning': then, it appears to me, it will again be inadequate for the construction out of it of any theory of understanding. That is, if it were possible to give an account of, for example, when two expressions have the same meaning, which did not overtly rely on an account of what it was to know the meaning of an expression, then it would not be possible to derive an account of knowledge of meaning from it. There is, indeed, good reason to suppose it impossible to give an account of synonymy save via an account of understanding, since it is a requirement on the former that whoever knows the meanings of two synonymous expressions must also know that they are synonymous: but I am saying merely that, if such an account of synonymy were possible, there would be no route from it to an account of understanding.

Any theory of meaning which was not, or did not immediately yield, a theory of understanding, would not satisfy the purpose for which, philosophically, we require a theory of meaning. For I have argued that a theory of meaning is required to make the workings of language open to our view. To know a language is to be able to employ a language; hence, once we have an explicit account of that in which the knowledge of a language consists, we thereby have an account of the workings of that language; and nothing short of that can give us what we are after. Conversely, it also appears to me that once we can say what it is for someone to know a language, in the sense of knowing the meanings of all expressions of the language, then we have essentially solved every problem that can arise concerning meaning. For instance, once we are clear about what it is to know the meaning of an expression, then questions about whether, in such-and-such a case, the meaning of a word has changed can be resolved by asking whether someone who understood the word previously has to acquire new knowledge in order to understand it now.

If a theory of meaning gives an account of the working of the language to which it relates, then, it seems, it must embody an explanation of all the concepts expressible in that language, at least by unitary expressions. We need not stop to inquire whether, or in what cases, someone who does not possess the linguistic means to express a concept, or who lacks a language altogether, may yet be said to grasp that concept: it is sufficient to acknowledge that the proto-typical case of grasping a concept is that in which this grasp consists in the understanding of a certain word or expression, or range of expressions, in some language. Hence, if a theory of meaning is a theory of understanding, as I have claimed, it would appear to follow that such a theory of meaning must, in explaining what one must know in order to know the meaning of each expression in the language, simultaneously explain what it is to have the concepts expressible by means of that language.

The theory of meaning will, of course, do more than this: it plainly cannot merely explain the concepts expressible in the language, since these concepts may be grasped by someone who is quite ignorant of that particular language, but who knows another language in which they are expressible. Hence the theory of meaning must also associate concepts with words of the language—show or state which concepts are expressed by which words. And an alternative view will be that it is only this latter task which properly belongs to the theory of meaning: that to demand of the theory of meaning that it should serve to explain new concepts to someone who does not already have them is to place too heavy a burden upon it, and that all that we can require of such a theory is that it give the interpretation of the language to someone who already has the concepts required. Let us call a theory of meaning which purports to accomplish only this restricted task a 'modest' theory of meaning, and one which seeks actually to explain the concepts expressed by primitive terms of the language a 'full-blooded' theory. One question which I wish to try to answer is whether a modest theory of meaning is possible at all, or whether anything to be ranked as a theory of meaning must be full-blooded.

If a well-known conception, propounded by Davidson, of the form which a theory of meaning ought to take be accepted, then, I think, it must be maintained that a modest theory of meaning is all that we have a right to ask for. On this conception, the core of the theory of meaning will be a theory of truth, framed on the model of a truth definition of Tarski's kind (the object-language not, in general, being assumed to be a fragment of the metalanguage): such a theory of truth will, however, lack the apparatus required for converting it into an explicit definition, and will not be serving to explicate the concept of truth in any way, but, taking it as already known, to give the interpretation of the object-language. The theory of truth will yield a T-sentence for each sentence of the object-language, viz. either a biconditional whose left-hand side is of the form 'The sentence S is true' or the universal closure of a biconditional whose left-hand side is of the form 'An utterance of the sentence S by a speaker x at a time t is true.' The notion of translation is not, however, appealed to in judging whether the T-sentences which the theory yields are the correct ones; rather, there are constraints which the theory must satisfy, to be acceptable, relating to the sentences held true by the speakers of the language (it being supposed that we can frame adequate criteria for whether a speaker holds a given sentence to be true): in the first place, that, by and large, the T-sentences derivable in the theory of truth state, on their right-hand sides, the conditions under which in fact the speakers hold true the sentences named on their left-hand sides.

The axioms of the theory of truth, when it forms part of the theory of meaning for a language under such a conception, will state the denotations of the proper names of the language, give the conditions for the satisfaction of the primitive predicates, etc. If a primitive predicate of the language expresses a certain concept, it would seem quite out of place to claim that a theory of meaning of this kind, or, in particular, the axiom of the theory of truth which governed that predicate, provided any explanation of that concept. Rather, the theory would be intelligible only to someone who had already grasped the concept. A Davidsonian theory of meaning is a modest theory.

I have already observed that a translation manual is to be contrasted with a theory of meaning, and cannot itself claim to be one. A theory of meaning describes directly the way in which the language functions, a translation manual merely projects that language on to another one, whose functioning must, if the translation is to be of practical use, be taken as already known. This point has equally been insisted upon by Davidson, who has put it by saying that the translation manual tells us only that certain expressions of the one language mean the same as certain expressions of the other, without telling us what, specifically, the expressions of either language mean; it would, he says, be in principle possible to know, of each sentence of a given language, that it meant the same as some particular sentence of another language, without knowing at all what meaning any of these sentences had. This objection to regarding a translation manual as itself constituting a theory of meaning is evidently just: but we may wonder why so heavy an emphasis is laid upon the distinction between a translation manual and a theory of meaning when the theory of meaning is required to be, not full-blooded, but only modest. A translation manual leads to an understanding of the translated language only via an understanding of the language into which the translation is made, an understanding which it does not itself supply; hence, we may say, it does not directly display in what an understanding of the translated language consists. But a modest theory of meaning, likewise, leads to an understanding of the object-language only via a grasp of the concepts expressed by its primitive expressions, which it does not itself explain; it seems, therefore, that we should similarly say that such a theory of meaning does not fully display in what an understanding of the object-language consists. Especially is this so since our best model—and, in many cases, our only model—for the grasp of a concept is provided by the mastery of a certain expression or range of expressions in some language. Thus a translation manual presupposes a mastery of some one other language—that into which the translation is made—if we are to derive from it an understanding of the translated language; but a modest theory of meaning presupposes a mastery of *some*, though unspecified, language, if we are to derive from it an understanding of the object-language. The significant contrast would, however, appear to be not between a theory which (like a translation manual) makes a specific presupposition and one which (like a modest theory of meaning) makes as heavy a presupposition, though less specific; but between theories which (like both of these) rely on extraneous presuppositions and those which (like full-blooded theories of meaning) involve no such presupposition at all.

Let us return to the question: should a theory of meaning issue in direct ascriptions of meaning? A theory of meaning should, of course, tell us, for each expression of the language, what it means: but it would be very superficial to conclude from this that it must therefore be possible to derive from the theory statements beginning 'The expression X means . . .' To give a trifling example, a successful theory of a crime, say a murder, should tell us the identity of the murderer: that does not entail that we should be able to derive from the theory a statement beginning, 'The identity of the murderer is . . .'; indeed (where 'is' is the sign of identity) there are no well-formed statements beginning that way. As a more serious example, we may note that 'chemistry' is not itself a concept of chemical theory. We do indeed require, of chemical theory, that it enable us to say which properties of a substance are chemical properties, which interactions are chemical ones, etc.; likewise, it may be required of a theory of meaning that it enable us to say which properties of an expression are semantic ones, that is, depend on and only on its meaning: but we cannot require that 'meaning' itself be a concept of the theory of meaning, at least if this is taken as entailing that we are enabled by it to characterize the semantic properties of an expression by means of a statement beginning 'The meaning of the expression is . . .' or 'The expression means . . .'

For expressions smaller than sentences, and particularly for connectives, prepositions, etc., there is some difficulty in framing even a grammatically correct form for a direct ascription of meaning (where, of course, we do not want to employ as the object of the verb 'means' a term denoting an expression, so that 'means' would become replaceable by 'means the same as'). However, it is not to my purpose to inquire how, or even whether, such difficulties may be resolved: we may restrict our attention to the case of sentences, for which the difficulty does not arise. Davidson himself allows that, from a theory of meaning of the kind he favours, a direct ascription of meaning will be derivable, at least for sentences. Given a T-sentence derivable from a theory of truth satisfying the required constraints, for instance the sentence ' "La terra si muove" is true if and only if the Earth moves,' we may legitimately convert it into what we may call an M-sentence, in this instance ' "La terra si muove" means that the Earth moves.' Now, earlier, we considered the question whether a theory of meaning which made no overt allusion to knowledge could nevertheless enable us to derive from it an account, for each expression, of what knowledge of the meaning of that expression consisted in; and, in particular, we supposed it argued that, if the theory allowed the derivation, for each expression, of a direct ascription of meaning, then it must also provide us with an account of what it was to know the meaning of a given expression, namely that this would be to know what was stated by the direct ascription of the meaning of the expression. But, now, if we are asked whether the M-sentence ' "La terra si muove" means that the Earth moves' expresses what someone has to know in order to know what the Italian sentence 'La terra si muove' means, we can hardly do other than answer affirmatively: to know that 'La terra si muove' means that the Earth moves *is* just to know what 'La terra si muove' means, for that is precisely what it does mean. If, on the other hand, we are asked whether an adequate account of what a knowledge of the meaning of 'La terra si muove' consists in is given by saying that one must know what is stated by the relevant M-sentence, then, equally, we are impelled to answer negatively: for the M-sentence, taken by itself, is, though by no means uninformative, signally unexplanatory. If these reactions are correct, then it follows that the fact that a theory of meaning issues in direct ascriptions of meaning is not in itself a sufficient ground for claiming that it gives an adequate account of what knowledge of meaning consists in.

One of our as yet unresolved problems was to discover what advantage a modest theory of meaning could have over a mere translation manual. A translation manual will inform us, for example, that 'La terra si muove' means the same as 'The Earth moves': but the inadequacy of this was said to lie in the fact that someone could know the two sentences to be synonymous without knowing what either of them meant. In order to derive, from a knowledge that the two sentences are synonymous, a knowledge of what the Italian sentence means, what someone has to know in addition is, obviously, what the English sentence means. Equally obviously, what, in addition to knowing the two sentences to be synonymous, has to be known in order to know that the Italian sentence means that the Earth moves, is that that is what the English sentence means. It follows that if we were to hold that a knowledge of the meaning of the Italian sentence consisted in knowing that it means that the Earth moves, we must also hold that knowing what the English sentence, 'The Earth moves,' means consists in knowing that *it* means that the Earth moves. An M-sentence such as ' "The Earth moves" means that the Earth moves,' for an object-language which is part of the metalanguage, appears totally unexplanatory because, this time, quite uninformative; although it still seems impossible to deny that someone knows what 'The Earth moves' means just in case he knows that it means that the Earth moves.

In this context, it is important to observe a distinction which, in many contexts, can be neglected: that between knowing, of a sentence, that it is true, and knowing the proposition expressed by the sentence. In using the phrase 'to know the proposition expressed by a sentence', I am intending no acknowledgement of propositions as entities, no commitment to an ontology of propositions: I employ the phrase simply as a convenient means of expressing the generalization of the distinction between, for example, saying of someone that he knows that the sentence '19 is prime' is true, and saying of him that he knows that 19 is prime. The reason why the M-sentence ' "The Earth moves" means that the Earth moves' appears quite uninformative is that it could not possibly be maintained that a knowledge of the meaning of 'The Earth moves' consisted in the knowledge that that M-sentence was true; for anyone who has grasped the simplest principles governing the use of the verb 'to mean', and who knows that 'The Earth moves' is an English sentence, must know that that M-sentence is true, even though he may not know what, in particular, 'The Earth moves' means. The case is analogous with Kripke's example of the sentence, 'Horses are called "horses".' Kripke says that anyone who knows the use of 'is called' in English must know that that sentence expresses a truth, irrespective of whether he knows what horses are: plainly, all he needs to know is that 'horse' is a meaningful general term of English, and, equally plainly, the relevant sense of 'knowing what horses are' is that in which it is synonymous with 'knowing what "horse" means'. Kripke allows, however, that someone who does not know what horses are will not know *which* truth 'Horses are called "horses" ' expresses. It seems reasonable to suppose that, by this concession, Kripke intends to deny that we could say of such a person that he knew that horses are called 'horses', although he is not explicit about this: that is, in my terminology, such a person may know that the sentence 'Horses are called "horses" ' is true, without knowing the proposition expressed by that sentence.

It might be objected that someone who knows a sentence to be true must also know the proposition expressed by the sentence, on the ground that if he knows enough about the meaning of the word 'true' to be credited with the knowledge that the sentence is true, he must know the connection between knowing something and knowing it to be true (and between believing it and believing it to be true, etc.); a connection which is displayed by the T-sentences. For instance, he must know that 'Horses are called "horses" ' is true if and only if horses are called 'horses': hence, since by assumption he knows that 'Horses are called "horses" ' is true, he will, if he is capable of performing a simple inference, also be capable of knowing that horses are called 'horses'. But this objection derives its plausibility from ignoring in its premiss the distinction which it purported to demonstrate to be without substance, that, namely, between knowing that a sentence is true and knowing the proposition it expresses. We may justifiably credit someone who does not know what 'horse' means, but who knows that it is a meaningful general term, with the knowledge that the T-sentence, ' "Horses are called 'horses' " is true if and only if horses are called "horses" ', is true: but to assume, as the argument requires, that he knows that 'Horses are called "horses" ' is true if and only if horses are called 'horses' is to beg the question.

To say of someone who does not know what 'The Earth moves' means, that he does not know that 'The Earth moves' means that the Earth moves, but only knows that the M-sentence is true, is not at all to say that he is not prepared to utter that M-sentence assertorically, but only the sentence, 'The sentence " 'The Earth moves' means that the Earth moves" is true.' It is not even to say that he could not give excellent grounds for the former utterance: on the contrary, he can give quite conclusive grounds, namely an appeal to the use of 'means' in English. But we have learned from Gettier's paradox that not every sound justification for a true belief is sufficient to entitle the holder of the belief to claim knowledge; the justification must be suitably related to what makes the belief true. A justification of an utterance of the M-sentence which would ground the ascription to the speaker of knowledge of the proposition expressed by that M-sentence would have to be one depending upon the specific meaning of the sentence of which the M-sentence treated, in our case the sentence, 'The Earth moves,' even though, in ordinary circumstances, no one would think of justifying such an utterance in so complicated a way.

All this shows that we were entirely right in our first inclination, to regard it as a necessary and sufficient condition of someone's knowing what 'The Earth moves' means that he know that it means that the Earth moves, that is, that he know the proposition expressed by the corresponding M-sentence. But it shows equally that we were also right to regard the M-sentence as being quite unexplanatory of what it is to know the meaning of the sentence, 'The Earth moves.' The simplest way we have to state its unexplanatory character is by observing that we have so far found no independent characterization of what more someone who knows that the M-sentence is true must know in order to know the proposition it expresses, save that he must know what 'The Earth moves' means: knowledge of that proposition cannot, therefore, play any part in an account of that in which an understanding of that sentence consists. And, if an M-sentence for which the metalanguage contains the object-language is unexplanatory, then an M-sentence for an object-language disjoint from the metalanguage is equally unexplanatory. In the latter case, the M-sentence does indeed provide some information: but the knowledge of the truth of such an M-sentence (as opposed to a knowledge of the proposition it expresses) does not require the possession of any information not also contained in the corresponding sentence from a translation manual.

The considerations about the connection between knowledge and justification which we saw to underlie the distinction between knowing the truth of a sentence and knowing the proposition expressed by it can be generalized to cases where it is not precisely this distinction which is in question. The expression 'knows that' is, of course, frequently used in everyday discourse, and in philosophical contexts in which attention is not focused on the concept of knowledge, merely as synonymous with 'is aware that'. Where 'knowledge' is used in a stricter sense, however, knowledge of a fact transcends mere awareness of it in that it involves that the awareness of it was arrived at in some canonical fashion, that is, that it was *derived* in some special way. If, then, we attempt to explain in what some capacity consists by saying that it consists in having a certain piece of knowledge, and if the plausibility of this account depends upon taking 'knowledge' in the strict sense, rather than as mere awareness, the attempted representation of the capacity will remain inadequate so long as it stops short at simply stating the *object* of knowledge—what it is that must be known, in the strict sense of 'know', for someone to have that capacity. To give an adequate explanation of the capacity in question, the account must do more than simply specify the fact that must be known: it must indicate how, in particular, awareness of that fact must have been attained, that is, what process of derivation is required for it to count as *knowledge*, in the strict sense.

It may be objected that no one has ever supposed that an adequate explanation of the meaning, or the understanding, of a sentence could be given by alluding merely to the M-sentence relating to it. In the terms in which I have just discussed the matter, the whole point of the theory of meaning is that it displays the canonical means by which the M-sentence is to be derived: only someone who was capable of so deriving it could be said to know it, in the strict sense, or, as I earlier expressed it, could be said to know the proposition it expresses. Such an objection is entirely just: my purpose in discussing M-sentences at such length was not to refute a thesis which no one has held, but to analyse the intuitive reasons we all share for rejecting such a thesis, in order to bring out some general points which we may apply elsewhere.

In order, then, to see in what, on a Davidsonian account, the knowledge of the meaning of a sentence consists, we must look to the way in which the M-sentence relating to it is derived in the theory of meaning. The M-sentence is, as we noted, obtained by replacing 'is true if and only if' in the corresponding T-sentence by 'means that': and the T-sentence is, in turn, derived from the axioms of the theory of truth governing the constituent words of the sentence and those governing the methods of sentence-formation exemplified by it. This, of course, entirely accords with our intuitive conviction that a speaker derives his understanding of a sentence from his understanding of the words composing it and of the way they are put together. What plays the role, within a theory of meaning of Davidson's kind, of a grasp of the meanings of the words is a knowledge of the axioms governing those words: in our example, these may be stated as ' "The Earth" denotes the Earth' and 'It is true to say of something "It moves" if and only if that thing moves.' (This latter formulation of the axiom governing 'moves' eschews appeal to the technical device of satisfaction by an infinite sequence, and is only an approximate indication of what is wanted: but, if we are intending a serious representation of what is known by anyone able to speak English, we cannot literally credit him with an understanding of that technical device.)

It is not sufficient, for someone to know what the sentence 'The Earth moves' means, for him to know the M-sentence relating to it to be true; he must know the proposition expressed by that M-sentence. And the natural way to characterize what, in addition, someone who knows the truth of the M-sentence has to know in order to know the proposition it expresses is: the meanings of the component words. If, now, we explain an understanding of the component words as consisting in a knowledge of the axioms of the theory of truth which govern those words, the same question arises: is it sufficient for him to know those axioms to be true, or must he know the propositions which they express? The objection to requiring only that he know the axioms to be true is parallel to that we allowed in the case of the M-sentence: anyone who knows the use of 'denotes', and who knows that 'the Earth' is a singular term of English, must know that the sentence ' "The Earth" denotes the Earth' is true, even if he does not know what, specifically, the phrase 'the Earth' means or what it denotes.

This might be objected to, however, on the ground that if we were to change the example from 'The Earth moves' to 'Homer was blind', it would become apparent that, in order to know that ' "Homer" denotes Homer' is true, one must know more than that 'Homer' is a proper name: one must know also that it is not an empty name. Such an objection is ill taken, because, for any language in which the possibility that 'Homer' is an empty name is open, the relevant axiom of the theory of truth will not take the simple form ' "Homer" denotes Homer'; at least, it will not do so if the name's being empty would deprive the sentence ' "Homer" denotes Homer' of truth. It is only in a theory of truth for a language of a Fregean type, in which all singular terms are so understood as to be guaranteed a denotation, that the axiom governing each proper name will take that simple form. For languages of other types, the axiom governing such a name as 'Homer' will have to take a different form. For instance, for any language in which the predicate '. . . is Homer' was taken as true of the referent of 'Homer', if any, and false of everyone and everything else, the axiom could take the form, 'For every x, "Homer" denotes x if and only if x is Homer.' If, now, the language was Russellian, so that the presence of an empty name in an atomic sentence rendered that sentence false, suitable further axioms would yield the T-sentence, ' "Homer was blind" is true if and only if Homer was blind.' If, on the other hand, the language was such that the presence of an empty name in a sentence, save when it followed the sign of identity, rendered that sentence neither true nor false, then we should not want that T-sentence to be derivable, since, if 'Homer' were an empty name, the left-hand side would be false while the right-hand side was not false. One would want, instead, the non-standard T-sentence, ' "Homer was blind" is true if and only if, for some x, x is Homer and x was blind.' Hence the demand that, in order to be able to derive the T-sentence relating to 'Homer was blind,' one would first have to know whether or not 'Homer' was an empty name, is quite unjustified.

This could be denied only if it were held that in order to know the meaning of 'Homer', one must know whether or not there was in fact such a man as Homer: for the theory of truth is a part of the theory of meaning for the language, and will embody all and only what is required for an understanding of the language. But, clearly, in order to know the use of the name 'Homer' in our language, it is not necessary to know whether or not it has a denotation: the most that could be required is that one should know whether or not it is known whether the name has a denotation. That is, it might be held that for a name for which it is known that it has a denotation, this knowledge enters into the understanding of the name: if so, then, for such a name, say 'London', the axiom governing it will take the simple form ' "London" denotes London.' A knowledge of whether 'Homer' has a denotation or not, on the other hand, cannot be part of what is involved in knowing the use of that name, for the obvious reason that this knowledge is not possessed by the speakers of the language.

If it is supposed that anyone attempting a serious inquiry whether there was such a place as London would thereby show that he was not in command of the accepted use of the name 'London', then it will be true that someone who knows of the word 'London' only that it is a proper name cannot yet recognize the axiom governing it to be true: he must also know that it is a name of which we are certain that it is not empty. But, plainly, one could be informed of this fact, and hence conclude to the truth of the sentence ' "London" denotes London,' without knowing what, precisely, 'London' meant; and so we must still conclude that a knowledge of the truth of the axiom is insufficient for an understanding of the name. It would be wrong to

112 M. A. E. Dummett

argue against this that merely to be informed that 'London' is a name known for certain not to be empty is not to *know* that fact, that to know it, in the strict sense, involves knowing specifically how the name 'London' is used. If such an argument were correct, then Davidson's objection to considering a translation manual as a theory of meaning, that one could, for example, know that 'la terra' means the same as 'the Earth' without knowing what either of them meant, would be unsound: for one could, in the same way, argue that while someone might be informed of their synonymy, he could not, in the strict sense, *know* it without knowing what both words meant. The objection would run foul of the methodological principle we have adopted, namely not to accept as part of an explanation a requirement that someone know something, where 'knowledge' is taken in the strict sense, as transcending mere awareness, but no account is given of what would constitute such knowledge.

It is essential to observe this principle if we are to avoid null or circular explanations. Suppose it true—doubtful as it seems to me—that one could not know, in the strict sense, that a name denotes a well-known object still in existence, without knowing the precise use of the name. This must be because, in order to count as *knowledge*, an awareness of the fact must be derived in a particular way. It is one of the merits of a theory of meaning which represents mastery of a language as the knowledge not of isolated, but of deductively connected, propositions, that it makes due acknowledgement of the undoubted fact that a process of derivation of some kind is involved in the understanding of a sentence. Where such a theory makes no appeal to any process of derivation is, naturally, in the recognition of the truth of the axioms. An insistence that such recognition amount to knowledge in the strict sense would, however, make a tacit appeal to a process by which their truth was derived, a process which the theory would fail to make explicit. It would, for example, be simply circular to say that an understanding of the name 'London' consisted in a knowledge, in the strict sense, of the truth of the sentence ' "London" denotes London,' and then go on to say that a condition for having such knowledge was a grasp of the precise use of the name: what we were seeking was a characterization of what constituted a grasp of the use of such a name.

There is thus no possibility of holding that an understanding of the component words of a sentence consists just in an awareness of the truth of the axioms governing them: one would have to know the

propositions expressed by those axioms. The theory of meaning must
therefore be capable of explaining what differentiates a knowledge of
the propositions expressed by those axioms from a mere awareness of
their truth. Now Davidson himself has fully recognized the obligation upon a theory of meaning to yield a theory of understanding: he
has been quite explicit about what, on his view, an understanding of
a sentence consists in, namely in a knowledge both of the relevant
T-sentence and of the fact that that T-sentence was derived from a
theory of truth for the language which satisfies the constraints imposed upon such a theory for it to be acceptable. The analogue, for
the understanding of a word, would presumably be a knowledge of
the axiom governing it and also of the fact that that sentence was an
axiom of a theory of truth satisfying those constraints. This time,
therefore, the suggestion is that we may represent a knowledge of the
propositions expressed by the sentences which serve as axioms as
consisting in an awareness of their truth supplemented by certain
background knowledge about those sentences.

It appears to me that only a very little consideration is needed to
recognize that this appeal to background information cannot supply
what we need. If someone does not know what 'the Earth' means, he
will learn something from being told that the sentence ' "The Earth"
denotes the Earth' is true, provided that he understands the verb
'denotes'; he will learn, namely, that 'the Earth' is a singular term and
is not empty. But if, now, he asks to be told the specific meaning of
the term, he will not be helped in the least by being told that the sentence in question is an axiom in a theory of truth for English satisfying certain particular constraints. Obviously, what tells him what,
specifically, 'London' denotes is the *sentence* ' "London" denotes
London' itself, and, in particular, the object of the verb 'denotes' in
that sentence, and not any extraneous information *about* that sentence. What is being attributed to one who knows English is not
merely the awareness that that sentence (and others like it) is true, but
that awareness taken together with an understanding of the sentence;
in other words, a knowledge of the proposition expressed by the
sentence. Of course, when we consider the degenerate case in which
the metalanguage is an extension of the object-language, the requirement that the metalanguage be understood becomes circular; in
order to derive from the axiom a knowledge of what 'London'
denotes, one would have already to understand the name 'London'.
But there is no requirement that the theory of truth be expressed in an

extension of the object-language: if the axiom ran ' "London" denota Londra,' then it would be an understanding of the term 'Londra' that was needed in order to learn the denotation of 'London', and there would be no circularity.

This is reasonable enough in itself, but it does not help us to understand what significant difference there is between a modest theory of meaning of this kind and a translation manual. It now appears clearly that we must ascribe to anyone able to use the theory of truth in order to obtain an interpretation of the object-language that he have a prior understanding of the metalanguage. This is even more apparent when we attribute to him an awareness that the theory of truth satisfies the required constraints, since these constraints allude to the conditions *stated* on the right-hand sides of the T-sentences, a notion which cannot be explained in terms of the formal theory, but presupposes an interpretation of it. Hence a theory of meaning of this kind merely exhibits what it is to arrive at an interpretation of one language via an understanding of another, which is just what a translation manual does: it does not explain what it is to have a mastery of a language, say one's mother tongue, independently of a knowledge of any other.

This conclusion could be avoided only if we could ascribe to a speaker of the object-language a knowledge of the propositions expressed by the sentences of the theory of truth, independently of any language in which those propositions might be expressed. If this is the intention of such a theory of meaning, it appears deeply dissatisfying, since we have no model, and the theory provides none, for what an apprehension of such propositions might consist in, otherwise than in an ability to enunciate them linguistically.

It may be replied that the apprehension of these propositions cannot be explained piecemeal, for each sentence of the theory of truth taken separately; but that a knowledge of the theory of truth as a whole issues, precisely, in an ability to speak and understand the object-language, so that there is no lacuna. What we are being given is a theoretical model of a practical ability, the ability to use the language. Since it is a theoretical model, the representation is in terms of the knowledge of a deductively connected system of propositions; and, since we can express propositions only in sentences, the model has to be described in terms of a deductively connected system of sentences. No presumption is intended that a speaker of the object-language actually has a prior understanding of the language in which those sentences are framed—that is why it is harmless to frame them in a language which is actually an extension of the object-language; but, equally, there is no undischarged obligation to say in what a grasp of the propositions expressed by the theory consists: it consists in that practical ability of which we are giving a theoretical model.

It is just here that the connection becomes apparent between a theory of meaning that proceeds via a theory of truth and a holistic view of language, a connection at first sight puzzling. A semantics which issues in a statement of truth conditions for each sentence, derived from finitely many axioms, each governing a single word or construction, appears at first as a realization of an atomistic conception of language, under which each word has an individual meaning and each sentence an individual content: the T-sentence for a given sentence of the language is derived from just those axioms which govern the words and constructions occurring in that sentence. But the connection between such a conception and the holistic view of language lies in the fact that nothing is specified about what a knowledge of the propositions expressed by the axioms, or by the T-sentences, consists in: the only constraints on the theory are global ones, relating to the language as a whole. On such an account, there can be no answer to the question what constitutes a speaker's understanding of any one word or sentence: one can say only that the knowledge of the entire theory of truth issues in an ability to speak the language, and, in particular, in a propensity to recognize sentences of it as true under conditions corresponding, by and large, with those stated by the T-sentences.

Thus the appeal to the knowledge that the theory of truth satisfies the external constraints does not serve to explain a speaker's understanding of any individual word or sentence, to bridge the gap between his knowing an axiom or theorem of the theory of truth to be true and his knowing the proposition expressed by it: it mediates merely between his knowledge of the theory as a whole and his mastery of the entire language. Now the allure of a theory of meaning of this type is that it appears to refute the suspicion that a holistic view of language must be anti-systematic; since to speak a language is to have the capacity to utter sentences of it in accordance with their conventional significance, there appears no hope of any systematic account of the use of a whole language which does not yield an account of the significance of individual utterances. A Davidsonian theory of meaning, on the other hand, combines the basic tenet of

116   *M. A. E. Dummett*

holism with what purports to be an account of the way in which the meaning of each individual sentence is determined from the meanings of its constituent words. This appearance is, however, an illusion. The articulation of the theory of truth is not taken as corresponding to any articulation of the practical ability the possession of which is the manifestation of that knowledge of which the theory is presented as a theoretical model. A speaker's knowledge of the meaning of an individual sentence is represented as consisting in his grasp of a part of a deductive theory, and this is connected with his actual utterances only by the fact that a grasp of the whole theory is supposed to issue, in some manner of which no explanation is given, in his command of the language in its entirety; but no way is provided, even in principle, of segmenting his ability to use the language as a whole into distinct component abilities which manifest his understanding of individual words, sentences, or types of sentence. To effect any such segmentation, it would be necessary to give a detailed account of the practical ability in which the understanding of a particular word or sentence consisted, whereas, on the holistic view, not only cannot a speaker's command of his language be so segmented, but no detailed description of what it consists in can be given at all. Hence the articulation of the theory plays no genuine role in the account of what constitutes a speaker's mastery of his language.

Against this it may be objected that the theory of truth does tell us something about the use of each individual sentence: for it states conditions under which a speaker will probably hold it to be true. Now it is certainly the case that a theory of meaning based on a theory of truth would reflect a molecular, rather than a holistic, view of language, if we could take the right-hand sides of the T-sentences as stating conditions under which speakers of the language invariably held true the sentences named on the left-hand sides. This is not a possible way of construing the theory, for two reasons. First, for any natural language, the conditions stated on the right-hand sides of the T-sentences will not, in general, be ones which we are capable of recognizing as obtaining whenever they obtain. A molecular theory of meaning based on the notion of truth conditions must attribute to one who understands a sentence a knowledge of the condition which must obtain for it to be true, not a capacity to recognize that sentence as true just in case that condition holds. Secondly, such an account would leave no room for mistakes. In order to leave room for them, we must claim that an acceptable theory of truth will give the *best possible* fit between the conditions for the truth of a sentence and the conditions under which it is held to be true, not a *perfect* fit: it follows that a speaker's understanding of a sentence cannot be judged save in relation to his employment of the entire language. (Indeed, it is somewhat dubious whether an individual speaker's mastery of the language can be judged at all. If we have identified a linguistic community from the outside, then a Davidsonian theory of meaning will give us a fairly good, though necessarily imperfect, guide to which sentences its members will hold to be true. There will be divergences on the part of the entire community—cases when we shall say, on the basis of that theory of meaning, that the community shares a mistaken belief. There will also be disagreements between individual speakers. How are we to discriminate between such a disagreement as may occur between two speakers who both tacitly accept the same theory of meaning for their common language, and one which reflects differing interpretations of that language? Presumably, if a member of the linguistic community holds a divergent theory of truth for the language, he will tend to diverge more in his judgements than most speakers do from the majority. But, since no finite set of such divergences will, in itself, reveal his reliance on a non-standard theory of truth, it is hard to see how either he or the other speakers or we as observers could ever detect this, or how, once discovered, it could be corrected. The difficulty arises precisely because there is no way of determining, within such a theory, the individual content with which any speaker endows a sentence.)

Davidson makes a virtue of necessity, and, as you heard in his brilliantly clear exposition in the first lecture in this series, uses the gap between the truth condition of a sentence and the condition under which it is held true to explain the genesis of the concept of belief. This is, however, an abnegation of what we are entitled to expect from a theory of meaning: such a theory ought to be able to distinguish between disagreements stemming from difference of interpretation and disagreements of substance (disagreements about the facts); it ought to be able to explain how it is possible for disagreement over the truth value of sentences to occur even when there is agreement over their meaning. We have, of course, been taught by Quine to regard this distinction with suspicion; and it is undeniably the case that the meanings of expressions of natural language are frequently fuzzy, and that the distinction becomes in consequence blurred. It is equally true that, as Davidson remarked in his lecture, we ought not lightly to assume that every disagreement over truth value, for instance of the sentence 'The Earth is round', should be regarded as one of substance rather than of interpretation. But a theory of meaning which denies in principle the viability of the distinction runs the risk of becoming solipsistic. A disagreement between individual speakers of the same language at the same time either cannot be accounted for at all, or should be explained by attributing to them divergent theories of truth for the language: and the same applies to a change of mind on the part of one individual. If the latter course is taken, we lose the conception of the linguistic community: a language, considered as determined by a theory of meaning, becomes something spoken by a single individual at a certain period.

The obvious fact of the matter is that the judgements which we make are not directly correlated with the states of affairs which render them true or false. Even if the correct theory of meaning for our language would represent our grasp of the meaning of each sentence as consisting in our knowledge of the condition which must hold for it to be true, we do not, in general, arrive at our evaluation of the truth of a sentence by direct recognition that the appropriate condition obtains, since, for the most part, that condition is not one we are capable of so recognizing. Should we therefore say that an adequate theory of meaning must be able to give an account not merely of what determines our judgements as correct or incorrect, but also of how we arrive at them, since this also depends upon the meanings we assign to the sentences whose truth value we are judging; and that this account must be able to show how, in the process, we are capable of going astray, even when we share with other speakers a common interpretation of the sentence? Whether we say this or not is partly a matter of taste, of how much we wish to reckon as belonging to a theory of meaning; such an account certainly belongs within a complete description of the workings of language. If a theory of meaning, based on a molecular view of language, enables a clear content to be given to an individual's associating a certain meaning with a sentence, a meaning which determines when that sentence may rightly be judged to be true, then we also have a clear criterion for when a judgement represents a mistake of fact; if we then choose to decree that an account of the processes leading to such mistakes does not belong to the theory of meaning, only a demarcation dispute is involved. But a theory of meaning based on a holistic view, which has no criterion for a speaker's associating a specific meaning with any one sentence, save his inclination to hold it true or false, and does not therefore purport to give an account of his understanding of that sentence, but only of the entire language, can give no determinate content to the notion of a mistake, which it invokes only to account for the lack of fit between the theory of truth and the judgements actually made by speakers. It would be absurd to expect a theory of meaning to ascribe to every expression a completely sharp meaning; I am arguing, however, that it is required that a place be left for a distinction between a disagreement of substance and a disagreement over meaning, a distinction which was not, after all, invented by mis-guided theorists, but is actually employed within our language. Any theory which associates sentences merely with truth conditions, with-out either attempting any account of the means by which we recog-nize or judge those truth conditions to be fulfilled, or providing any means of determining that an individual speaker, or even the whole community, associates a particular truth condition with a particular sentence, save a rough agreement between the truth conditions of all sentences under a given theory and the judgements made concerning them, is incapable of providing any place for such a distinction.

Now it could be replied that I am quite wrong in denying that Davidson can represent an individual speaker's grasp of the meaning of a particular sentence: in the lecture that inaugurated this series, he stated that an individual's understanding of a sentence consisted in his knowing, of the relevant T-sentence, that it was derivable from some theory of truth, satisfying the required constraints, for the lan-guage, without his having actually to know that theory of truth. But how is it to be judged that an individual knows this? What, indeed, is he to do with the information if he has it? It might be claimed that he will manifest this knowledge by judging that sentence to be true just in case the condition stated in the T-sentence obtains. But why should he do this? Well, it may be said, he knows that the theory of truth which yields that T-sentence achieves the best fit with the judgements made by other speakers, and he wants to maximize the agreement of his judgements with theirs. It is true, by hypothesis, that this theory of truth will achieve the best fit possible *for a theory of truth*: but since it will not achieve a perfect fit, he would do better, in maximiz-ing agreement, not to be guided exclusively by any theory of truth. How can he know that he would not achieve a better agreement by disregarding the theory of truth in this instance? After all, it cannot be the case that other speakers all follow the policy of judging the truth values of sentences only in accordance with the given theory of truth, otherwise the fit *would* be perfect: so why should he? To this it can only be replied that the other speakers do try to follow that policy, but make mistakes in doing so. We have now come round once more to the question: what is a mistake? In attributing to the speakers a policy of conforming their judgements to a theory of truth, we have surreptitiously ascribed to them a capacity for judging whether the truth conditions of sentences are fulfilled—judgements which will not always be correct; but we have given no content to the notion of such a judgement, as distinct from a judgement as to the truth value of a sentence.

That we should appeal to the notion of a mistake in order to explain the lack of fit between a theory of truth and the actual judgements made by speakers of the language sounds plausible only because we find the notion of such a mistake already intelligible: we are familiar enough with the idea that someone may assign a determinate meaning to a sentence, and yet wrongly judge it to be true. But a theory which offers no explanation of how such mistakes occur has no right to appeal to this notion. We can see this plainly if we consider any theory which does not have language as its subject-matter, for instance, a physical theory. It would not be tolerable, for example, to say that a theory of the motions of the planets was one that achieved the best possible fit with their observed movements, any discrepancy being due to mistakes on the part of the planets. If all we had to go on, in constructing a theory of meaning, were judgements of speakers as to the truth or falsity of sentences, and the conditions prevailing when those judgements were made, then we should be entitled to demand, of any theory we were asked to accept, that the fit be perfect, save for small discrepancies assignable to errors of observation. Fortunately, this is not all that we have to go on.

The upshot of our discussion therefore, is this. If a theory of meaning of this type is taken literally, as relating to a theory of truth framed in actual sentences, it has no advantage over a translation manual, since it has to presuppose an understanding of the metalanguage. If, on the other hand, it is construed as attributing to a speaker an unverbalized knowledge of the propositions expressed by the sentences of the theory, its explanatory force evaporates, since it provides no means whereby we can explain the ascription to an individual of a knowledge of the various distinct propositions and their deductive interconnection. That is to say: a modest theory of meaning either accomplishes no more than a translation manual, and hence fails to explain what, in general, someone knows when he knows a language; or it must be construed holistically, in which case its claim to give a systematic account of the mastery of a language is spurious, since a holistic view of language precludes the possibility of any such account.

We have noted that a theory of meaning, if it represents an understanding of an expression as consisting in the possession of a certain piece of knowledge, cannot rest content with specifying the object of this knowledge, and insisting that 'knowledge' must be taken in a strict sense; it must also display the way in which that knowledge had to be derived in order to qualify as knowledge. But our more recent considerations have related to a different point. In many contexts, we may take as unproblematic the ascription to someone of awareness of some fact, since we may credit him with an understanding of language, and the manifestation of his awareness will consist primarily in his ability to state the fact or his propensity to assent to a statement of it. But, where we are concerned with a representation in terms of propositional knowledge of some practical ability, and, in particular, where that practical ability is precisely the mastery of a language, it is incumbent upon us, if our account is to be explanatory, not only to specify what someone has to know for him to have that ability, but also what it is for him to have that knowledge, that is, what we are taking as constituting a manifestation of a knowledge of those propositions; if we fail to do this, then the connection will not be made between the theoretical representation and the practical ability it is intended to represent. I am not objecting to the idea of a theoretical representation of a practical ability as such, and certainly not to the representation of a mastery of a language by means of a deductive theory: I am saying only that such a representation is devoid of explanatory power unless a grasp of the individual propositions of the theory is explained in terms of a specific practical capacity of the speaker. I do not know whether this is possible; I do not know that holism is an incorrect conception of language. But I am asserting that the acceptance of holism should lead to the conclusion that any systematic theory of meaning is impossible, and that the attempt to resist this conclusion can lead only to the construction of pseudo-theories; my own preference is, therefore, to assume as a methodological principle that holism is false.

The next question that naturally arises is whether a full-blooded theory of meaning could be given in terms of the notion of the truth conditions of a sentence: you will be relieved to hear that I shall spare you the extended discussion that an answer would demand. But we are in a position to deal briefly with another question about the form which a theory of meaning should take, namely whether, in terminology which I borrow from Mr. John McDowell, it should be rich or austere. If the theory of meaning is given in terms of truth conditions, then, where a proper name is concerned, a rich theory will attribute to a speaker who understands the name a knowledge of the condition which must be satisfied by any object for it to be the bearer of the name, while an austere theory will simply represent him as knowing, of the object for which the name in fact stands, that it is the bearer. For this case at least, namely where the theory is framed in terms of truth conditions, the distinction appears to coincide with that between a full-blooded and a modest theory, although it is differently formulated. For a more verificationist type of theory, an austere theory will credit anyone who understands a name with a capacity to recognize its bearer when encountered, whereas a rich theory will, instead, represent him as ready to acknowledge whatever is taken as establishing, for any given object, that it is the bearer. In favour of the rich theory, it might be said: 'We don't *simply* recognize objects: we recognize them *by* some feature.' It might be replied, on behalf of the austere theory, that *how* we recognize an object is a psychological matter, irrelevant to a theory of meaning, and that, in any case, there does not have to be a means by which we recognize them; no one could give much of an account, for example, of the means by which he recognizes the predicate '. . . is red' as applying to something. So let us suppose that we encounter some rational but non-human creatures who have a language which contains what appear to be names of rivers: though they identify rivers under these names with remarkable accuracy, we cannot discover the means by which they make such identifications, nor can they give any account of this. It nevertheless remains that if one of these creatures has identified two distinct stretches of water by the same river-name, and it is subsequently proved, by tracing their courses, that there is no flow of water from one to the other, then he must withdraw one or other identification; at least, if these creatures do not acknowledge this necessity, then their words cannot be taken as names *of rivers*. So-called theories of reference are theories about what, in problematic cases, we should take as establishing which object, if any, was the bearer of a given proper name, and hence should more accurately be called theories of sense for proper names: the fact that they are so disputable shows how inexplicit our grasp of our own use of proper names is. But if our imaginary creatures use names in such a way that, in a case of disagreement, they would not accept as settling the question which object was the bearer whatever we should in fact so accept, then they do not understand these names in the way that we understand ours. Such examples bring out sharply the merit of the idea that what determines the meaning of a word is not so much what in practice normally prompts its application as what is agreed on as conclusively establishing its correct application in cases of dispute: to argue that we do not need to rely, on ordinary occasions of use, on any principle guiding us to apply it, is to miss the point of this familiar idea.

I conclude, therefore, that a theory of meaning, if one is to be possible at all, must accord with an atomistic, or at least a molecular, conception of language, not a holistic one; that it must be full-blooded, not modest, and rich, not austere. It need not issue in any direct ascriptions of meaning; but it must give an explicit account, not only of what anyone must know in order to know the meaning of any given expression, but of what constitutes having such knowledge. As I remarked, the next step would be to ask whether such a theory of meaning should be based upon the notion of truth conditions or upon some other notion. When I began composing this lecture, I had the absurd idea that I should have the time to go on to discuss not only that, but also the question raised by Professor Strawson in his extremely interesting inaugural lecture, concerning the relation between theories of meaning as we have been discussing them and the account of meaning given by Grice, and so to conclude by examining the notion of a linguistic act and the relation between such acts and their interiorizations, for example between assertion and judgement. Only by treating of these topics could one claim to have answered the question I have taken as my title: but, you will be glad to know, I thought it best not to try to complete the answer now.

APPENDIX

It is helpful to view a Davidsonian theory of meaning by contrasting it with Frege's theory of sense and reference. Frege had two kinds of argument for the necessity of a notion of sense alongside the notion of reference. The first relates to the knowledge of a language by a speaker, and consists, fundamentally, in the observation that it is unintelligible to attribute to anyone a piece of knowledge of which the *whole* account is that he knows the reference of a given expression; if someone knows what the referent of an expression is, then this referent must be given to him in some particular way, and the way in which it is given constitutes the sense which he attaches to the expression. The way to understand this argument is as follows. To attribute to someone a knowledge of the reference of, say, the name 'Oxford' is to say of him that he knows, of the city of Oxford, that it is the referent of that name. To say of him that he knows the reference of the name, without attaching any particular sense to it, is to say that the *complete* account of his possessing this piece of knowledge is given by saying that he knows, of the city, that it is the referent of the name; and this amounts to saying that this piece of knowledge cannot be further characterized by saying of him something of the form, 'He knows that the city which . . . is the referent of "Oxford".' Likewise, to attribute to someone a knowledge of the reference (extension) of, say, the predicate '*x* is supple' is to say of him that he knows, of those things which are supple, that the predicate is true of them: while to say that he knows the reference of the predicate, without attaching any particular sense to it, is to say that this attribution constitutes a *complete* account of this particular piece of knowledge; and this amounts to denying that that piece of knowledge can be further characterized by saying of him anything of the form, 'He knows that "*x* is supple" is true of any object which . . .'

That is to say, an attribution to someone of a knowledge of the reference of an expression is to be understood as a statement of the form ⌜*X* knows, of *a*, that it is *F*⌝, or of the form ⌜*X* knows, of the *G*s, that they are *F*⌝, that is, a statement in which the subject of the 'that'-clause stands, in a transparent context, outside the 'that'-clause; let us call such a statement an 'attribution of knowledge about an object or objects'. And the assertion that someone knows the reference of an expression without attaching to it any particular sense amounts to attributing to him knowledge about an object, or objects, while denying that there is any further characterization of that piece of knowledge by means of a statement of the form ⌜*X* knows that *b* is *F*⌝, or ⌜*X* knows that the *G*s are *F*⌝, that is, one in which the subject of the 'that'-clause appears within it and hence in an opaque context; let us call such a statement an 'attribution of propositional knowledge'. But, according to the Fregean argument, an attribution of knowledge about an object or objects is unintelligible if accompanied by the claim that no further characterization, in terms of propositional knowledge, is possible. For, on this view, propositional knowledge is basic: whenever an attribution of knowledge about an object or objects is correct, there must be some correct attribution of propositional knowledge from which it follows. Hence there can never be such a thing as *bare* knowledge of the reference of an expression, that is, knowledge of the reference unmediated by any sense which is attached to the expression.

It should be noted that this argument, as stated, does *not* entail the so-called 'description theory of names', which its opponents tendentiously ascribe to Frege. The 'causal theory of names', for instance, itself proffers an account of the condition which an object must satisfy to be the bearer of a name. The crucial disagreement between the causal theory and the description theory is not over whether any such condition exists, but over whether it is possible to state it without essential reference to the name itself. (The attribution of the description theory to Frege is tendentious because there is no argument which he advanced which purported to show that this is always possible.)

For all that this line of argument can show, the sense which each speaker attaches to an expression might be different, even though each must attach *some* sense to it. Frege's second line of argument concerns the contribution which is made to our non-linguistic knowledge, at the time when we first recognize it as true, by a sentence which we understand. This argument is most familiar in application to identity-statements: if, in order to understand a proper name, a speaker has to know, of the referent, that it is the referent, then it is incomprehensible how a true identity-statement $\ulcorner a = b \urcorner$ can convey new knowledge to him, since he must already know, of the object which is the referent of the two names, that it is the referent of each of them. Actually, the argument works just as well for any atomic statement: on the above assumption about names, and on the corresponding assumption that, in order to understand a predicate, a speaker must know, of each object of which the predicate is true, that the predicate is true of it, it is equally incomprehensible how a true statement formed by inserting a name in the argument-place of a predicate can convey new information to him. If we suppose that an account of the use of language in communication demands that each sentence possess a common cognitive content for all speakers, then this argument does provide a ground for ascribing to each expression a sense constant from speaker to speaker.

The conclusion of the first argument is, in effect, that we need to ascribe to a speaker *more* than just a bare knowledge of the reference of each expression, whereas the conclusion of the second argument is that if sentences are to be informative, we cannot, in general, attribute to speakers *as much as* a knowledge of the reference of expressions. There is no real tension here. If we merely require, for someone to be said to know of an object x that it is the referent of the name N, that there be some term t which stands for x and is such that it is true to say of that person ⌜He knows that t is the referent of N⌝, then it does *not* follow that someone who knows, of a certain object, both that it is the referent of one name and that it is the referent of another, that he knows that the names have the same referent; on the contrary, we have here in schematic form precisely the account in terms of sense which Frege proposes as the solution of the problem. The supposition which the second argument seeks to reduce to absurdity is, rather, that an understanding of an expression consists in a *bare* knowledge of the reference. What it adds to the first argument is just a ground for thinking that sense must be common to different speakers.

Now at first sight Davidson's theory is one which explains everything in terms of reference, without bringing in sense; but this first appearance is quite misleading. Davidson's attribution to a speaker of an (implicit) knowledge of the proposition expressed by the axiom governing the name 'Oxford' does not consist in holding that that speaker knows, of the city of Oxford, that the name 'Oxford' denotes it, but, rather, that he knows that 'Oxford' denotes the city of Oxford. Thus Davidson is certainly not attributing to each speaker a *bare* knowledge of the reference of each expression that he understands, in the sense in which Frege's arguments tell against such an attribution. (I did, in the lecture, interpret McDowell's notion of an austere theory of meaning as involving a bare knowledge of the reference. This was probably a misinterpretation of McDowell's intention.)

The question indeed arises exactly *what* knowledge we attribute to a speaker when we represent him as knowing that 'Oxford' denotes Oxford, given that we want to attribute more to him than just the trivial knowledge of the truth of the sentence ' "Oxford" denotes Oxford': and here we are inclined to say that Davidson's theory is modest in that, while it does not fall foul of Frege's arguments by ascribing to speakers a bare knowledge of reference, but allows that they attach particular senses to expressions, it does not attempt to explain what these senses are. This is essentially the line which I took in the lecture when I was criticizing the notion of a modest theory of meaning; although, when I came to consider Davidson's holism, I was inclined to take it as entailing that no account of sense could be supplied.

Subsequent reflection has, however, suggested to me that this may not have been the right line to take. What is a modest theory of meaning? Is it one which leaves room for an account of the senses which speakers attach to their words (the concepts they associate with them), but which does not itself provide such an account? Or is it a theory which denies in principle the possibility of giving any such account? If we take Davidson's theory as modest in the former sense, then the possibility remains open of filling it out with an account of the specific senses speakers attach to the words of the language, and thus converting the theory into a full-blooded, atomistic one: but, in that case, what becomes of the holistic aspect of the theory? Such holism as remained would relate only to the description of the way in which a theory of meaning for a language which, initially, one did not know might be arrived at from an observation of the linguistic and other behaviour of the speakers: in devising a theory of meaning, one would have to fit the theory to all the evidence provided by the judgements of speakers as to the truth and falsity of their sentences. Holism in respect of the evidence for a theory of meaning is, however, a quite different thing from the holistic view of language of which I spoke in the lecture. The latter concerns the theory of meaning itself, not the way in which a non-speaker might arrive at it; specifically, it relates to the account that is given of the way in which an implicit grasp of the theory of meaning, which is attributed to a speaker, issues in his employment of the language, and hence, as I argued, in the content of that theory. Holism merely in respect of how one might, starting from scratch, arrive at a theory of meaning for a language, on the other hand, has, in itself, no such implications, and is, so far as I can see, unobjectionable and almost banal. It is certain that Davidson intends his holism as a doctrine with more bite than this.

Davidson might subscribe personally to a tendentious doctrine of holism, even though his conception of a theory of meaning was, in itself, neutral as between a holistic, a molecular, and an atomistic view of language; but it is unlikely that there is no more organic a connection between the different features of his philosophy of language. If, on the other hand, we take his theory of meaning as being modest in the second of the two senses indicated above, it becomes difficult to see how it differs from a theory which repudiates the notion of sense altogether, and ascribes to the speakers a bare knowledge of the references of their words. The conclusion to which I am driven is that it is, after all, a mistake to view a Davidsonian theory of meaning as a modest one in any sense. Let us see how this can be.

There are many different kinds of consideration which have been adduced in favour of linguistic holism: the most relevant for our purpose is that which generalizes Wittgenstein's observations about the name 'Moses'. Wittgenstein's thesis is that there are a number of things which we ordinarily believe to be true of Moses—that he was brought up in a royal palace, that he led his people out of slavery, that he delivered the Law to them, etc., etc. No one of these has to continue to be held true, on pain of our losing the use of the name 'Moses': provided that we continue to believe that there was just one man of whom a large number of those things are true, we may reject the rest. Here it may be allowed that we attach more weight to some things we believe about Moses than to others; as far as the determination of the bearer of the name is concerned, we may attach no weight at all to some of them. Wittgenstein treated only of the case in which we are concerned with determining the referent of a single name; but it is plain that we may adapt it to that in which we are concerned with the simultaneous determination of the referents of two names, say 'Moses' and 'Aaron'. There are a number of sentences containing one name or the other which we regard as true, some of which, such as 'Moses and Aaron were brothers,' contain both. We may now make some such stipulation as the following. If there exists a unique pair of individuals, m and a, such that, when these are taken as the respective referents of 'Moses' and of 'Aaron', a (weighted) majority of the sentences containing 'Moses' come out true, and also a (weighted) majority of the sentences containing 'Aaron' come out true, then these individuals are the actual referents of the names. If there is no such pair, or more than one such pair, but there is a unique individual m such that, when m is taken as the referent of 'Moses' and all sentences containing 'Aaron' are taken as false, a (weighted) majority of the sentences containing 'Moses' come out true, then m is the actual referent of 'Moses', while 'Aaron' lacks a referent; and correspondingly for the case in which 'Aaron' has a referent but 'Moses' is empty. If none of these cases obtains, both names lack a referent.

I am not advocating such a doctrine; but it is readily intelligible, and has an obvious plausibility. On this account, the sense of a proper name is such that we have provided in advance that any one of the things which we regard as partially determinative of the referent may prove false, without the name's being deprived of reference. That does not, of course, mean that when we repudiate as false something that we had formerly regarded as true and as in part determinative of the reference, the sense of the name undergoes no alteration; on the contrary, it does so, because we no longer count the rejected statement among those a majority of which must be true of the bearer of the name.

The plausibility of Wittgenstein's account is not restricted to personal proper names; it is natural to apply it also to words of other kinds, for example mass terms. We arrive at a form of holism if we generalize the thesis simultaneously to all words in the language, including predicates, with the sole exception of the logical constants and perhaps prepositions and the like. Suppose that we have some large class (T) of sentences considered as true and as jointly determinative of the references of our words (names and predicates). Suppose also, as a large simplification, that we are given a determinate universe of objects over which the predicates may be taken as defined and within which the denotations of the names will fall. We now consider all possible *total assignments* of references to the names and predicates of the language: each such total assignment will constitute an interpretation of the language, relative to the given universe, in the sense of the standard semantics for a classical first-order language, save that a total assignment may allow that one or more names have no referents; it will assign referents to the other names, and extensions to the predicates. Any one total assignment will determine truth values for the atomic sentences of the language, and the valuation will be extended to all sentences via those axioms of the theory of truth which govern the sentence-forming operators. We may now specify the actual referents of the names and the actual extensions of the predicates to be those which they have under the *preferred* or *correct* total assignment, this latter notion being in turn explained in some suitable manner in terms of the class T. The simplest explanation, and the one which a holist would be most likely to favour, would be to say that the preferred total assignment is that

130 *M. A. E. Dummett*

unique one (if any) which brings out true a maximum number of sentences of T.[1]

If we now interpret Davidson's theory of meaning as incorporating a holistic account, along these lines, of how the references of the primitive non-logical words of the language are determined, we can no longer regard it as lacking an account of a speaker's grasp of the senses of those words: on the contrary, what a speaker implicitly knows is that reference is determined in this holistic manner. Such knowledge enters into the speaker's knowledge of the propositions expressed by the axioms of the theory of truth. For instance, what a speaker knows when he knows that 'Oxford' denotes Oxford is, on this account, that 'Oxford' denotes that object which is assigned to the name 'Oxford' under the preferred total assignment to the names and predicates of English; what he knows when he knows that 'x is supple' is true of an object if and only if that object is supple is that 'x is supple' is true of an object if and only if that object belongs to that set of objects which is assigned as the extension of 'x is supple' under the preferred total assignment; what he knows when he knows that 'The Earth moves' is true if and only if the Earth moves is that 'The Earth moves' is true if and only if that object which is assigned to 'the Earth' under the preferred total assignment is a member of that set which is assigned to the predicate 'x moves' under that assignment.

[1] An explanation more faithful to the original Wittgensteinian model would have to be rather complicated. We could say that a total assignment was *admissible* if, for each word to which it assigns a referent, it brings out true a majority of the sentences in T which contain that word, and call the *degree* of an assignment the number of names to which it assigns a referent; the preferred total assignment could then be stipulated to be that unique admissible assignment, if any, which is of maximal degree among admissible assignments. The complexity of this formulation seems to be unavoidable, if the pattern set by the case of just two interconnected proper names, such as 'Moses' and 'Aaron', is to be followed. For consider a case in which we have two such proper names, 'a' and 'b', and just five sentences containing them which we hold true, 'Fa', 'Ga', 'Rab', 'Hb', and 'Kb'; I assume the extensions of the predicates fixed. Suppose that there are just four individuals, i, j, m, and n, which are candidates to be the referents of these names, that i and m are in the extension of 'F', m alone in the extension of 'G', j and n in the extension of 'H', and n alone in the extension of 'K', while the pair $\langle i, j \rangle$ is the only one standing in the relation denoted by 'R'. Then if we assign i to 'a' and j to 'b', two of the three sentences containing 'a' come out true, and two of the three containing 'b' come out true; but exactly the same result is obtained by assigning m to 'a' and n to 'b'. We should want, in this case, I suppose, to say that the indeterminacy deprived the names 'a' and 'b' of reference; there would be no ground for ruling that just *one* lacked a reference, since we should have no basis for deciding which.

Looked at in this way, a Davidsonian theory appears as ineradicably holistic, but no longer as in any sense a modest theory: so regarded, it goes unscathed by complaints, such as I made in the lecture, that the theory gives no account of what the knowledge that is attributed to the speakers of the language consists in. I should still argue that the whole conception of a modest theory of meaning is misbegotten; but I think that the impression, which not only I but, I believe, a number of Davidson's supporters had, that a theory of meaning of his kind is to be interpreted as a modest one, is to be rejected. A large part of the reason for so interpreting it lies in the fact that Davidson has always represented the collection of data about the judgements actually made by speakers as to the truth and falsity of sentences as standing in a relation of *evidence* to the resulting theory of truth; whereas, on the holistic conception of sense which I sketched above, they do not provide external support to the theory, but are integral to it. For consider the model from which we started, Wittgenstein's account of the name 'Moses'. Someone who has no idea *which* sentences containing the name 'Moses' are generally held to be true, but who knows merely that the name denotes that unique individual, if any, of whom a majority of those sentences, whatever they are, are true, would not be said by Wittgenstein to grasp the use of the name 'Moses': he merely has a correct schematic account of the form which a specification of its use—or that of any other name—must take. In order to know the specific use of the name 'Moses', he must know which particular sentences involving the name are generally held true. Admittedly, individual speakers frequently exploit the existence of an established use for a name or other word, holding themselves responsible to the established means for determining the application of the word without themselves having a complete mastery of it; this often applies strikingly to place-names. This is a consequence of the fact that a language is a social phenomenon rather than a family of similar idiolects, and does not affect the fundamental point. To be able to use a name, or other word, at all, otherwise than in the fashion of a recording apparatus, a speaker must know something specific about the way its reference is determined, even if he does not know everything relevant; and the fact that there is a socially established application to which he holds himself responsible depends upon there being a means of discovering what governs that application.

In the same way, on a holistic theory, a man cannot be said to know the axiom governing 'the Earth', that is, to know that 'the Earth' denotes the Earth, if he merely knows that the expression denotes that object which is assigned to 'the Earth' under that total assignment to the primitive expressions of English which brings out true the maximum number of sentences generally held true by English speakers, whatever those sentences may be. In knowing that, he knows only the general schema in accordance with which the particular explanation of the use of any singular term, in any language, must be given, and, in addition, no more than that 'the Earth' is a singular term of English; he could have that knowledge without knowing anything more about the English language whatever, and could hardly, in such a case, be said to know what 'the Earth' meant, or, therefore, the proposition expressed by ' "The Earth" denotes the Earth.' In order to know the specific meaning of 'the Earth', to know the proposition expressed by that axiom, he must know which particular sentences make up the class T, relative to which it is determined which total assignment is the preferred one. (The holism comes out in the fact that it is the same specific piece of knowledge which is required for a grasp of the senses of all names and predicates of the given language.) Thus what Davidson calls the 'evidence' for the theory of truth is actually internal to it. The theory is not something that we base upon the 'evidence', but which can be understood without knowing what the evidence for it may be: we cannot grasp or convey the content of the theory without explicit mention, in detail, of the sentences which jointly determine the references of our words; for without such mention, we cannot tell what references the theory of truth asserts those words to have.

My primary interest, in the lecture, was to arrive at certain basic principles regulating the construction of a viable theory of meaning; and most of those conclusions stand, even if I was mistaken in construing Davidson's conception of a theory of meaning as a modest one. One important conclusion, however, requires reconsideration, namely, that the adoption of a holistic view of language renders the construction of a systematic theory of meaning impossible. That now depends upon whether a Davidsonian theory, interpreted in the holistic manner sketched above, is or is not credible. The first impression, which is, I believe, a correct one, is that even if it is in principle coherent, it simply is not credible. We saw that to state the principles underlying the simultaneous determination of the references of two proper names in a Wittgensteinian manner was fairly complex: but in that context, the senses of the other words occurring in the various sentences containing those names were being taken as already known; and, because of the assumed fixity of the applications of general terms, the results of an inquiry as to the referents of the proper names, and, accordingly, the truth values of the sentences containing them, could be thought of as able to be *stated* by the use of general terms. But when we try to take seriously the idea that the references of all names and predicates of the language are simultaneously determined together, it becomes plain that we are thereby attributing to a speaker a task quite beyond human capacities. In such a simultaneous determination, there is no reason why the reference of any one word should prove to be such as to bring out true the maximum number of sentences of T containing that word; but, even if it were so, the speaker would derive little guidance from the thought that the referent of a name was that individual of whom the majority of the predicates extracted from such sentences were true. This would afford him little guidance, because he could not take it as already given what it was for any one such predicate to be true of any particular individual: on the contrary, that would be up for determination at the same time, via the determination of the extensions of the primitive predicates occurring in those sentences, and, ultimately, of all those in the language. For the same reason, the outcome of the process of determining the reference of any word could never be stated verbally, except perhaps when the referent was a possible object of ostension, since the words that might be used for stating it could not be taken as having an application given in advance of the determination of the reference of the word in question. Admittedly, while a conclusive demonstration of the truth of any one sentence would require that the task of discovering the referents of its constituent words under the preferred total assignment should actually be accomplished, the making of a single judgement as to truth value need not wait upon that task, any more than a judgement concerning Moses has to wait upon a definitive decision as to which of the things we normally believe about him are true; one might indeed infer from the holistic theory that no conclusive demonstration of truth could ever be provided. The fact remains that just as, on Wittgenstein's theory, one must know both how the referent of 'Moses' is determined, and the particular things we believe concerning Moses, in order to know the content of any sentence containing that name; so, on the holistic theory, one must both know the composition of the entire totality T, and have the conception of a simultaneous determination of the references of our words in relation to it, in order to grasp the content of any single sentence.

The difficulty of making the holistic account plausible becomes more apparent when we inquire into the composition of the base totality T. It would be somewhat contrary to the spirit of holism to admit that there exists a special class of privileged sentences, among all those generally considered true, which we might call 'quasi-analytic': sentences which are not individually immune to revision (although the rejection of any of them will effect a change in the senses of our words), but which play a special role, which other sentences acknowledged as true do not, in the determination of the references of our words. The holist nevertheless faces a choice, in the exact formulation of his doctrine, over whether or not he is to allow for disagreements between speakers. If he does not, then he must regard T as comprising just those sentences which all speakers accept as true, or, at least, which many accept as true and none rejects as false, and, therefore, as including only sentences having no significant indexical feature. But in this case it becomes implausible that T will be adequate to determine the application of many predicates, for instance of '. . . is supple': although most English speakers would agree on any one particular application of such a predicate, there are just too few actual sentences containing the word, whose truth most speakers would acknowledge, to determine its extension. In the face of this difficulty, the holist is more likely to make the other choice, and regard the base totality T as consisting not of sentences, but, rather, of individual judgements of truth value made by particular speakers. In this case, T will contain not only divergent judgements concerning non-indexical sentences, but also judgements relating to sentences with indexical elements, or, more accurately, to statements (where a statement is taken as a triple of a sentence, a speaker, and a time). This choice, however, involves a different implausibility: where T is taken as the totality of all judgements actually made by speakers of the language, no one speaker will come anywhere near having a grasp of the correct theory of meaning for that language, since the vast majority of those judgements will be unknown to him.

In order to escape this absurdity, the holist is subject to a strong temptation to shrink the notion of a language down to that of an idiolect; each individual speaker is now to be conceived as having his personal theory of truth for the language as he speaks it, a theory which incorporates, in its base totality T, all the judgements which he personally makes, but none of other speakers, since they are irrelevant to his idiolect. Such a conception inverts the true relation between the notion of an idiolect and that of a language, in the everyday sense of 'language'. A language, in the everyday sense, is something essentially social, a practice in which many people engage; and it is this notion, rather than that of an idiolect, which ought to be taken as primary. We cannot, indeed, dispense with the notion of an idiolect, representing an individual's always partial, and often in part incorrect, understanding of his language; but it needs to be explained in terms of the notion of a shared language, and not conversely. One among many reasons for holding this is the phenomenon called by Putnam the 'linguistic division of labour'; but it is unnecessary here to pursue the point in detail, since the shift from a common language to an idiolect does not extricate the holist from his difficulty.

If a speaker's mastery of his language consists in an implicit grasp of a theory of meaning for that language, then, if the theory is holistic, he must be aware of the judgements which comprise the base totality. Even when the language is his own personal idiolect, therefore, that totality cannot contain a multitude of casual judgements which he has made but has subsequently forgotten; it can, at any given time, contain only such judgements as can be elicited from him at that time. This still makes it grossly improbable that the totality can be sufficiently extensive to determine the references of all the words in his language.

Of certain words, it is perfectly reasonable to maintain the thesis that the reference of each of them is determined by the requirement that one or more sentences containing it should come out true. Wherever it can be held that there is an essentially unique way of defining a word, this fact can be expressed by applying that thesis to a single sentence incorporating the definition; and the thesis may be applied to any other word which must, or even may, be introduced by means of a verbal explanation, whether or not that explanation amounts to an actual definition. The description theory of proper names derives the considerable plausibility that it possesses precisely from the fact that proper names may be, and often are, introduced to someone who does not know them by means of a verbal explanation; and this fact also underlies Wittgenstein's account of the name 'Moses', which, as Kripke has observed, is a modification of the description theory. The modification has two features: first, it allows for the fact that there is usually more than one legitimate way of introducing a proper name, and that these different ways, taken together, supply more than is needed in order to determine its reference; and, secondly, it provides in advance for the resolution of any conflict that may emerge between the alternative means of fixing the referent. This account may, again, be represented by the thesis that the reference of such a name is determined by the requirement that a weighted majority of the sentences which might be used in introducing it should be rendered true. Among general terms, some behave in this respect like proper names, while, for some others, there are no multiple criteria for their application which could come into conflict, but, rather, essentially only one correct way of explaining them. Others, again, occupy an intermediate position: their explanation is complex, in the sense that one could represent their extension as being determined by the requirement that a number of different sentences should come out true; but the conflict which would be provoked by the discovery that it was impossible to maintain all these sentences, hitherto taken as constitutive of their meaning, would be much more severe than in the case of a name like 'Moses', and the means we should adopt for resolving such a conflict is not provided for in advance.

It is, undoubtedly, a fallacy to suppose that one may always simply equate the sense of what is said in explanation of a word with the sense of that word; and, whatever may be thought in detail of Kripke's views on proper names, they serve to underline the fallacy: to the extent that there is a generally understood difference in the employment of a definite description and of a proper name, the hearer will make a tacit allowance for that difference when a proper name is introduced to him by means of a definite description. Such a concession does not, however, invalidate the idea that the means we should employ for conveying to someone the sense of a word he did not previously understand displays the sense which it bears in the language, where grasping the sense of a word is equated with understanding its accepted use. If, for instance, there exists an established means of fixing the reference of a name, it will necessarily be integral to the sense of that name.

The thesis that reference is determined by the requirement that all, or most, sentences in a certain set should come out true may thus be sustained in respect of a large number of words. It loses its plausibility, however, when it is generalized by the holist to apply to all the words of the language simultaneously. This is because it was, in the first place, a particular way of representing the sense of a word which it is possible to introduce by means of a verbal explanation: its plausibility therefore extends so far as it is applied only to words which may be so introduced, and maintained only in relation to those sentences which could legitimately be used in giving such an explanation. If a speaker's grasp of the sense of a word is to be represented as consisting in his knowledge that its reference is determined by a set of sentences containing that word, then those sentences must be ones that might actually be elicited from him in explaining the word; and, if we are considering the word as part of a common language, then they must be sentences generally accepted as true and also as determinative of the sense of the word, that is, as legitimate to cite in explanation of its sense. The holist is therefore wrong to include, in his base totality T, judgements particular to individual speakers, or ones which an individual speaker does not remember making or would not allude to in explaining a word to someone who did not understand it. It follows that the thesis that the references of our words are determined by the requirement that certain sentences be true cannot be generalized, as the holist wishes to generalize it, to provide an account of how the references of *all* words in the language are fixed: there are many words in the language which are not, and cannot be, introduced by means of purely verbal explanations, and to these the thesis simply does not apply. Our language is a many-storeyed structure, and the possibility of introducing new expressions —into the language or into the vocabulary of a particular speaker— by means of linguistic explanations depends upon our first constructing the lower storeys by different means; notoriously holism is at its weakest in the account that it gives of the progressive acquisition of language. But a correct theory of meaning is required to give an account of what it is to have a mastery of a language *at all*: a model which gives a representation only of how, by the use of a fundamental part of the language, one may come to grasp the senses of expressions at higher levels is a bad general model to employ in constructing such a theory.

As we have already seen, the judgements made by individual speakers play a dual role on Davidson's account: on the one hand, they form the evidence which might be used by someone with no prior knowledge of the language who was wishing to construct a theory of meaning for it; on the other, they become an ingredient of the theory itself, as making up the totality T which determines the references of the words. In the former role, no objection can be levelled against the appeal which is made to them: if we are trying to discover, from observation of someone's linguistic behaviour, the sense which he attaches to a certain word, we shall naturally pay attention to all the judgements of truth value which he makes in regard to sentences containing that word, since such judgements obviously display the propensity which he has to employ that word in a certain manner. But the idea that we can then, by reference to the totality of all judgements made by speakers, obtain a single uniform representation of the manner in which the bearers of all the names and the extensions of all the predicates of the language are determined, overlooks the diversity of the many types of expression our language contains, and the gradations of level at which they lie. This may seem a hard saying, in face of the fact that it was Quine, the principal modern exponent of linguistic holism, who advanced the celebrated image of language as an articulated structure, whose sentences lie at differing depths from the periphery; but the fact is that that image in no way represents an essentially holistic view of language, and, indeed, accords rather badly with such a view. For holism, language is not a many-storeyed structure, but, rather, a vast single-storeyed complex; its difficulties in accounting for our piecemeal acquisition of language result from the fact that it can make no sense of the idea of knowing part of a language. As in the present case, the insights which provide the starting-points for arguments to a holistic view are perfectly genuine; holism results from succumbing to the temptation to generalize them beyond their range of application, in order to arrive at a single formula to cover every case.

7 Names and Identity

P. T. GEACH

I TAKE my start from a sentence in the preface to Frege's *Begriffs-schrift*: 'I believe that the replacement of the concepts *subject* and *predicate* by *argument* and *function* is going to approve itself with time.'[1] The simplest application of the Fregean apparatus in logic is to take a name as argument, and a proposition as the corresponding value, of what we may call a linguistic function. (As in other works of mine, I use 'proposition' in the medieval sense: for a sentence serving, as grammarians say, to express a complete thought, to say what is or is not so, rather than for the thought so expressed.) When propositions are values of one and the same function for different names as arguments, we may say that we have the same predication made about different objects named by the different names.

With such a set of examples as 'Brutus killed Caesar', 'Cato killed Caesar', 'Caesar killed Caesar', which Frege would regard as values of one and the same function for the arguments 'Brutus', 'Cato', and 'Caesar' respectively, there is no manifest advantage in his way of speaking over the older way of speaking, over describing the propositions as got by attaching a common predicate 'killed Caesar' to three different subject-terms; and thus far it might appear that Frege had merely found new labels to tag onto the constituents of a proposition that would previously have been labelled 'subject' and 'predicate'. But this appearance is dispelled by considering certain other very simple cases, such as we find in Frege himself. Consider the examples 'Brutus killed Brutus', 'Cato killed Cato', 'Caesar killed Caesar'. Intuitively it is clear that what the first proposition predicates of (the man) Brutus, the second predicates of Cato, and the third, of Caesar: truly in the first two cases, falsely in the third. And it is also

[1] p. xiii.

clear that to this saying of the same thing there corresponds in the realm of language a common mode of forming the propositions. But here the old analysis into subject and predicate terms does not apply: there is no common word or expression that can be picked out to be the common predicate.

It may be objected that these examples could be rephrased, in better English, as 'Brutus killed himself', 'Cato killed himself', and 'Caesar killed himself', and then we would have a visible common predicate, 'killed himself'. This answer is quite insufficient. If 'himself' were just a pronoun of laziness, to avoid inelegant repetition of words, then 'killed himself' could not logically be treated as one common predicate in the three sentences. This admits of positive demonstration. Let us imagine a slightly modified form of English in which 'ditto' is used as a pronoun of laziness: and suppose one of the rules for its use goes like this:

Every A is R to ditto iff every A is R to every A.

This rule is of course far from a complete characterization of the use of 'ditto': it tells us only how to understand 'ditto' in one kind of context. All the same, the rule is clear and self-consistent, and in fact I shall not need to lay down further rules for 'ditto'. For it is clear already, if *this* rule holds, that '(is) R to ditto' cannot lawfully be treated as a common predicate in the propositions in which it figures: so to treat it would continually bring out false conclusions from true premises. Consider the valid schema:

Every A is a B or is a C
Every B is P; every C is P
Ergo: Every A is P.

If 'is R to ditto' were a genuine form of predicate, we could easily establish that this was a valid form of argument:

Every A is a B or is a C.
Every B is R to every B.
Every C is R to every C.
Ergo: Every A is R to every A.

For one would only need to turn two of the premises into the 'ditto' form, infer a conclusion by the schema I have just given, and finally eliminate the 'ditto' from the conclusion by the rule.

What this shows, I repeat, is not that the rule for 'ditto' is itself objectionable; however, once we have laid down the rule, it is not within our power to stipulate whether 'is *R* to ditto' is a genuine form of predicate; it just is not, whatever we stipulate. On the other hand 'is *R* to itself' *is* a genuine form of predicate; but it is so only because already, without regard to the possibility of introducing expressions of this form, 'Brutus killed Brutus' and 'Caesar killed Caesar' and 'Cato killed Cato' predicate the same thing of Brutus, Caesar, and Cato respectively. Someone who wants any deep insight into linguistic structure must train himself to discern a common predication, even in cases like this where there is not a string of words identifiable as the common predicate; and he must make this a matter of direct discernment, not of what they call 'putting propositions into logical form'. My three examples are of course logically quite in order just as they stand, and do not need to be *put* into logical form; and just as they stand they already show that they predicate one and the same thing of three different men. So, for that matter, do these three: 'Nobody except Brutus loved Brutus', 'Nobody except Caesar loved Caesar', 'Nobody except Cato loved Cato.' And here the replacement of 'Brutus', 'Caesar', and 'Cato' at their second occurrence by 'himself' would be wrong.

People have a recurrent doubt whether 'is *R* to itself' does express a genuine form of predicate: are not reflexive paradoxes notorious? I shall here say only that in my view these paradoxes arise from the particular subject-matter—set theory or semantics, say—and not just from the reflexive construction: ordinary first-level predicate calculus runs into no inconsistencies on account of reflexivity. Again, as some readers of my *Reference and Generality* have protested, if we say that there is a common predication in 'Nobody except Brutus loved Brutus' and 'Nobody except Caesar loved Caesar', then we seem to be shifting from the domain of language to the domain of what language signifies. The protest is misconceived; the common pattern of the two propositions, readily discerned, is still linguistic—a feature of language, though not an extractable bit of language—and we may now see the point of dropping the old analysis into two pieces, a subject and a predicate, in favour of Frege's idea of a proposition-forming operation upon names.

Of course some very simple propositions consist of two terms, which may be labelled 'subject' and 'predicate'. But in 'Raleigh smokes', let us say, the two terms have totally different modes of significance. 'Raleigh' signifies just by being a man's name. We cannot sensibly ask what 'smokes' names; what is significant is not the bare word 'smokes' but a certain pattern—name followed by 'smokes'. And speaking of a common pattern in 'Raleigh smokes', 'Churchill smokes', etc., is just another way of saying what Frege would have expressed by saying we had values of a common function for a series of different arguments—the names 'Raleigh', 'Churchill', etc. It is another question whether to this function from names to whole propositions there corresponds a non-linguistic function, taking as its arguments the men Raleigh, Churchill, etc.—and what the values of this function will be. Happily I need not go into that now.

I want to emphasize that Frege's problems and difficulties about function are not to be escaped by a manœuvre of semantic ascent. It is a common, and a silly, criticism of Frege to suggest that his distinction between object (*Gegenstand*) and function is a misconstrual of the category-difference between two kinds of expression, for example between numerals like '2' and functors like 'log'. If we consider—as Frege of course did consider—such examples as '$2^2, 3^3, 4^4 \ldots$', we see that what signifies the function is not a separably displayable functor, but the common pattern or rule of formation: and this brings us back to Fregean functions and arguments—to a function whose values for the numerals '2, 3, 4 . . .' as arguments are the expressions '$2^2, 3^3, 4^4 \ldots$'. And then we see that in 'log 2' what signifies is not the bare word 'log' but the pattern got by writing it to the left of a numeral. Frege's alleged confusion is no confusion; the proposed remedy for it is no remedy; and the idea of a function is needed even to talk about linguistic structures, so the attempt to get away from it by semantic ascent is futile.

Language, after all, is not something set over against the whole world, like the Divine Mind; languages are part of the world, linguistic facts and structures are facts and structures in the world. This sets a limit to the usefulness of semantic ascent in solving philosophical problems. We cannot solve the problem of universals by talking about the word 'pig' instead of The Pig; for there is exactly the same problem about the relation of the word 'pig' to its tokens as there is about the relation of The Pig to Jones's pigs. We cannot solve the problem about the synthetic incompatibility of red and green by saying that it is a matter of our deciding never to call the same thing 'red' and 'green'; such a decision would be idle if one and the same utterance could have the sound of 'red' and of 'green'. (The Anglo-

Saxons were surely in bad trouble when they had two words, one meaning 'black' and the other 'white', but both sounding something like 'black'.) So also in our case; the business of function and argument and value cannot be shelved by talking about expressions of different category, because it reappears if we consider, as we must, the ways of forming expressions out of expressions. No proper explanation is possible; the matter can only be presented and talked around, in the hope that some people will catch on; that they have caught on is shown by their command of simple logical apparatus. We are down to bedrock, and the spade turns if we try to dig deeper.

There may still appear to be problems about subject and predicate that the Fregean analysis cannot satisfactorily answer. I have described the difference between the two terms in 'Raleigh smokes' by saying that 'Raleigh' has the role of a name, whereas 'smokes' has significance merely as serving to form this pattern: a name followed by 'smokes'. But why should we not contrariwise say that 'smokes' has significance as the name of an activity, smoking, whereas 'Raleigh' has significance merely as serving to form this pattern: 'Raleigh' followed by the name of an activity—a pattern common to 'Raleigh smokes', 'Raleigh drinks', 'Raleigh curses', and 'Raleigh sleeps'? Following Ramsey, Strawson raises this question; but he has quite a wrong idea how to answer it. Strawson supposes that the assertoric force of the proposition attaches somehow to the predicate term; but predication is effected just as much in moods other than the indicative, in questions, in unasserted clauses of asserted propositions. And Ramsey's doctrine has been developed, in a way I can only deplore, by the followers of Montague: if I understand them aright, they would rehabilitate the theory assimilating 'somebody' and 'nobody' to proper names, since 'Raleigh smokes', 'Somebody smokes', and 'Nobody smokes' would alike make predications concerning the activity of smoking.

I argued years ago, and I still hold, that the unequivocal way of telling which of two terms in a simple predication is a name and a logical subject is to consider negation. If we represent such a simple predication schematically as 'Fa', then we may write its negation as '$\sim Fa$', using no brackets: it makes no difference whether we regard negation as operating on the predicate-term 'F' and giving us a negated predicate '$\sim F$', or as operating on the whole proposition 'Fa'. First-order predicate logic consistently ignores any difference between '$(\sim F)a$' and '$\sim(Fa)$', in both senses of the word 'consistently'

—that this is constant practice, and that we can be sure no inconsistency arises from this.

For names the matter is totally different. Of course we could write '*aF*' instead of '*Fa*', and '*~aF*' instead of '*~Fa*'. But if we then tried treating '*~a*' as a syntactically coherent substring of '*~aF*', and as an expression with the same syntax as the name '*a*', substitutable for '*a*' *salva congruitate* in all contexts, then we should speedily get into contradictions. I argued this in *Reference and Generality*;[1] but my argument had the weakness that I assumed certain properties of conjunctive predications, which an obstinate follower of Ramsey or Montague might deny sooner than give up the idea that a name is as predicative and as much negatable as what is vulgarly considered a predicate. I had in reserve, however, an argument free from this assumption, and leading to the same conclusion as the one I published.

Let us suppose that a negation of '*a*', '*~a*', can stand *salva congruitate* wherever '*a*' can stand; and let us suppose that however we interpret '*F*', '*~aF*' is a predication contradicting '*aF*'. Now let us consider the propositional form '$(\sim a)R(\sim a)$'! Using Frege's Greek-consonant gap-fillers, we see this is the way '*~aF*' comes out if we read 'ξF' as '$\xi R\xi$': so we get:

(1) $(\sim a)R(\sim a) \longleftrightarrow \sim(aRa).$

But '$\sim(aRa)$' is also the way '*~aF*' comes out if we read 'ξF' as 'ξRa': and in terms of *this* interpretation of 'ξF' we shall have:

(2) $\sim(aRa) \longleftrightarrow (\sim a)Ra.$

Finally, let us compare together '$(\sim a)Ra$' and '$(\sim a)R(\sim a)$'. If '*a*' and '*~a*' really are mutually substitutable in all contexts *salva congruitate*, then '$(\sim a)R\xi$' will be a legitimate reading of 'ξF', just as '$aR\xi$' is; and in terms of *this* reading of 'ξF' we get:

(3) $(\sim a)R(\sim a) \longleftrightarrow \sim((\sim a)Ra).$

But (1), (2), (3) form a patently inconsistent triad, of the form '$p \longleftrightarrow \sim q, \sim q \longleftrightarrow r, p \longleftrightarrow \sim r$'.

There's glory for you, as Humpty Dumpty would say: there's a nice knock-down argument! But this sort of glory for the author rarely carries immediate conviction to the reader; it is well for mankind that it is so, or we would constantly be deceived by the subtle fallacies of sophists. So I now consider a series of possible objections.

[1] Cornell University Press, 1962, p. 32 f.

First, have I not been careless about brackets—treating '$\sim aF$' as though it could be read indifferently as '$(\sim a)F$' or as '$\sim(aF)$'? But this is exactly the point: you can be careless with brackets in '$\sim Fa$', or rather brackets are needless and meaningless; the whole success story of first-order predicate logic shows this; therefore if you may not happily be careless about brackets in '$\sim aF$', this is enough to show that negation attaches to predicates in a way it does not attach to names.

Secondly, I reached my formulas (1), (2), and (3) by using each time a new reading of 'ξF' in the paradigm '$(\sim a)F \longleftrightarrow \sim(aF)$'. Can this be legitimate? I mention this objection because it has a little history: it has been used to show that one of Russell's set-theoretical paradoxes simply arises from wrong and mutually inconsistent substitutions. Russell considers that relation which a relation R bears to a relation S iff R is not self-related to S: let us call this relation 'T', then we have:

(4) R is T to S iff R is not R to S.

But now if we substitute 'T' for 'R', we at once get, whichever relation S is:

(5) T is T to S iff T is not T to S.

The objection, which keeps on being raised again—as Lewis Carroll said, one may postulate that a finite line of argument, that is, one already finished and disposed of, may be produced to any extent in subsequent discussion—is that in (4) the letter 'T' stands in for 'not R', so that it is no wonder if we arrive at a contradiction if we are replacing 'T' with 'R' in formula (4) to get (5). Logicians have rightly held that the paradox of non-self-relating relations is not cracked all that easily. You might as well argue that the following proof in propositional logic is unsound:

$$\vdash p \to (q \to p)$$
$$Ergo: \vdash \sim p \to (q \to \sim p)$$

because we replaced the 'p' of the first line by '$\sim p$' in the second line. And the feeling of discomfort produced by my tricky threefold substitutions is not a whit better founded.

Thirdly, Ramsey would protest at my analysing 'aRa' now on the result of reading 'ξF' as '$\xi R\xi$', and now as the result of reading 'ξF' as

'ξRa'. For Ramsey argues that that means we regard the proposition 'aRb' as being an 'incomprehensible trinity' of propositions, of which one asserts that the relation R holds between a and b, the second asserts the possession by a of the complex property of 'having R to b', while the third asserts that b has the complex property that a has R to it. These must be three different propositions because they have three different sets of constituents, and yet they are not three propositions but one proposition, for they all say the same thing, namely that a has R to b.[1]

If we indeed could not analyse one and the same proposition in different ways, then, as Frege remarked, logic would simply be crippled; but Ramsey's difficulty is only specious.

The resolution of the difficulty points up the advantage of Frege's function–argument apparatus over the old subject–predicate account. If a proposition were analysable into a predicate and one or more subjects—these being actual expressions, and constituents of the proposition—then one might well expect that, failing ambiguity of syntactical construction, as in 'Drinking chocolate is nice', the analysis will be unique. But one and the same number may be the value of one function for one argument, of another function for another argument, and of a two-argument function for a certain pair of arguments: the number 16 is the value of the square function for the argument 4, the value of the function 4^ξ for the argument 2, and the value of the function $\xi . \zeta$ for the arguments 2 and 8. Nobody would now ask which it is *really*, or talk of an incomprehensible trinity. And this is the analogy Frege would have us bear in mind. If we suppose definite meanings attached to 'a', 'R', and 'b', then one pattern of propositions is given by 'ξRb' — 'aRb, bRb, etc.'; a second by '$aR\zeta$' — 'aRa, aRb, etc.'; and a third by '$\xi R\zeta$'—all the propositions thus far listed are instances of this pattern: 'aRa, aRb, bRa, bRb, etc., etc.' The proposition 'aRb' comes on all three lists: it illustrates all three patterns, is a value of three different Fregean functions; why not?

I conclude then that the thesis of *Reference and Generality* is correct: in a two-term predicative proposition, only one of the two terms has a predicative role, only one can be regarded as combining with negation to form a term of the same kind and with the effect of negating the whole proposition. Various views opposed to this thesis are to be rejected: Ramsey's view that either term may be taken as subject, and the 'Montague' grammarians' view that 'Raleigh',

[1] F. P. Ramsey, *Foundations of Mathematics and Other Essays*, ed. R. B. Braithwaite, London, 1931, p. 118.

'somebody', and 'nobody' are all to be assimilated as predicates, since each can be attached to what would vulgarly be called a predicate, e.g. 'smokes', but is here regarded as a subject. Moreover, even when we seem to have a quotable piece of a sentence that can be picked out as a predicate, the significant thing is not this bit of verbiage but a sentence-pattern that it serves to form.

In this last conclusion I am opposing the view put forward recently by Dummett in his book on Frege. Consciously diverging from Frege, Dummett puts out a distinction between simple predicates and complex predicates: the account of predication that I have given would I think be acceptable to Dummett as regards complex predicates but not as regards simple ones. This difference between simple and complex predicates is not a matter of number of words, but of quotability. The common predicate in 'Brutus killed Brutus' and 'Caesar killed Caesar' is not to be exhibited by quoting a common piece of the two propositions; it can be exhibited only by some such device as the Fregean 'ξ killed ξ', or Quine's equivalent device of circled numerals, or again by writing '—— killed ——', but stipulating that the same name must fill both blanks; in all three cases, what stands between quotes is not a physical part of the sentence in which the common predicate occurs. But Dummett thinks that the word 'smokes' in 'Raleigh smokes', or the word 'hit' in 'Tom hit Bill' and 'John hit Mary', is itself quotable as a simple predicate. The distinctive features that mark off simple predicates from names on the one hand and complex predicates on the other are explained by Dummett in a passage I find remarkably obscure; to be fair, I shall give it verbatim.

[I]t is to the simple predicates and relational expressions that we must assign slots into which singular terms have to be fitted, rather than ascribing to the singular terms slots into which the predicates and relational expressions have to be fitted. But this does not make the simple predicates incomplete in the sense that Frege intended when he spoke of incomplete expressions. We might say that in the case of simple predicates the slots are external to them, whereas in the case of complex predicates, they are internal. That is, we can know what linguistic entity, considered as a sequence of phonemes or of printed letters, a simple predicate is, without knowing anything about the slot it carries with it: the slot consists merely in the predicate's being subject to a certain rule about how it can be put together with a term to form a sentence. But the complex predicate cannot be so much as recognized unless we know what slots it carries: they are integral to its very being.[1]

[1] Michael Dummett, *Frege, Philosophy of Language*, London, 1973, p. 32 f.

Obviously we cannot in fact recognize a predicate in a sentence simply from the occurrence therein of a sequence of phonemes or printed letters: such a sequence may not be a word at all, or may not be the right word; the point is so obvious and so trite as not to need illustration. But even if we suppose the simple predicate to be easily recognized, it is clear that Dummett's account is inadequate and his departure from Frege a mistake. Let us take one of his examples, the verb 'killed'. We certainly cannot understand the use of this if we do not understand the difference between 'John killed Mary' and 'Mary killed John'. The different sense of the relation if John killed Mary, and if Mary killed John, is shown by there being a relation between linguistic entities, which likewise can hold either from the name 'Mary' to the name 'John' or the other way around; as regards English, this relation is represented by the predicate:

The name ξ is written just before, and the name ζ just after some token of the word 'killed'.

Word order is not the only relation that will serve this purpose, and we may be misled by concentrating on it. For example, Polish is an inflected language, and for Polish the relation between proper names corresponding to the relation of killing borne by one person to another would be represented by the predicate:

The name ξ in the nominative case, and the name ζ in the accusative case, are combined with a token of the word 'zabił', inflected to agree in gender with the name ξ.

And if we think of this sort of example, surely the temptation vanishes to regard the predicate in the Polish sentence 'Maria zabiła Jana', the verb 'zabiła', as a simple sign with its slots for proper names quite external to it: the predication is effected by the function 'ξ zabił(a) ζ', not by the bare word 'zabił' or 'zabiła'.

In the last paragraphs there is a certain linguistic awkwardness, of some philosophical interest. It is natural to speak of the function 'ξ killed ζ', or the two-place predicate 'ξ killed ζ': but here, as Frege would put it, by a kind of linguistic necessity we cannot quite say what we are trying to say. The function 'ξ killed ζ' obviously is not identifiable with the actual expression, containing Greek consonantal letters, that I have just written down within quotes: and if we speak of the predicate 'ξ killed ζ' as figuring in 'John killed Mary' or 'Mary killed John', then again what we quote does *not* figure in these sen tences. The actual expression 'ξ killed ζ' is neither a function nor a predicate: it serves however to identify a two-place predicate shared by many sentences, and this is the same thing as identifying a function yielding such sentences as 'John killed Mary' and 'Mary killed John' as its values when proper names are supplied as its arguments. One well acquainted with Frege will recognize that we have here a reduplication on the linguistic level of Frege's difficulties about the concept *man*. There is nothing in the least surprising about this; if I am not mistaken, Frege himself foresaw the difficulty's arising on the linguistic level too.[1] Once again we see the futility of trying to escape Frege's difficulties by semantic ascent, by talking about words instead of the objects and concepts signified.

To return to Dummett's doctrine of simple predicates: Dummett remarks that Frege 'clearly stated that the sense of a complex expression has to be regarded as made up of the senses of the constituent words':[2] and when Dummett comes on to treat of senses as objects, we find that he treats the sense of a sentence as compounded out of the senses of its constituent words; these senses themselves are for Dummett again objects, as he explicitly says.[3] It is quite true that Frege did use the way of speaking cited by Dummett, but this way of speaking should to my mind be charitably expounded, not imitated.

Anyhow, if we do follow Frege here, we do well to follow him further, in regarding some 'constituents' of a sense as not objects but functions. The sense of 'The Earth is not flat' is the negation of the sense of 'The Earth is flat': we have here not a newly added constituent sense, the sense of the word 'not', but a function—the function *the negation of*—which gives a thought as its value for a thought as its argument.[4] Similarly in *On Concept and Object* Frege explicitly says, having in mind the senses of relational expressions: 'not all the parts of a thought can be complete; at least one must be "unsaturated" or predicative; otherwise they would not hold together.'[5] The senses of '2', 'is greater than', and '3', if all regarded as objects, would in Frege's words 'hold aloof from each other': it is only because the predicate 'is greater than' determines a two-place function, whose value for the sense of '2' and the sense of '3' as arguments is the

[1] See the footnote on page 46 of *Translations from the Philosophical Writings of Gottlob Frege*, trans. P. T. Geach and M. Black, Oxford, 1952.
[2] Op. cit., p. 25.
[3] Op. cit., p. 294.
[4] Geach and Black translation, pp. 131–5.
[5] Ibid., p. 54.

150   *P. T. Geach*

thought that 2 is greater than 3—it is only so, Frege would hold, that there can be such a thing as this thought, that the sense of '2 is greater than 3' exists as a unity at all.

I am not concerned, as Dummett is, to defend Frege's doctrine that senses are identifiable objects: but the only form of this doctrine that will get off the ground is the one clearly held by Frege himself—that what corresponds in the realm of sense to an incomplete expression, like 'not' or 'is greater than', is not an object, a complete sense, but a function with senses as its values and senses as its arguments. Dummett gives no account that I can follow of what makes the senses of names and simple predicates stick together to form a thought; and even if he had an account, it would be on the face of it inferior to Frege's, because not organically connected as Frege's is with the general doctrine of functions.

These remarks on Dummett's work should not be taken as indicating my general view of his book. There is a very large measure of agreement between Dummett and myself both about how Frege should be expounded and about which parts of Frege's theory of language are still tenable and which must be abandoned. But Dummett's doctrine of simple versus complex predicates is not merely, as Dummett puts it, a distinction that Frege himself was at no great pains to make; it is a radically un-Fregean distinction, which cannot be allowed without bringing Frege's fundamental insight into ruinous confusion. Fortunately it plays only a minor part in Dummett's exposition; and I have attacked it here only because the value justly ascribed to Dummett's account of Frege might get unjustifiably ascribed to this unsound element.

There is a doctrine of Frege himself that might be used to overthrow my thesis that names, unlike predicates, are not negatable. It is well known that Frege held that sentences are complex names of truth values: so the phrase 'it is not the case that . . .', which is a functor applicable to sentences and yielding sentences, would be a name-forming operator upon names. Moreover, Frege held that a functor taking names in its argument-place must be so explained that it yields an expression with a sense and a reference *whatever* name we insert. At this rate, since '2' and '2 > 3' are both names, 'it is not the case that 2 > 3' will be a name and also 'it is not the case that 2' will be a name. In *Grundgesetze* there is in fact a commitment to use of a symbol that could be read as 'it is not the case that 2';[1] and the

[1] Vol. I, p. 11.

Satzklang of this reading is not a misrepresentation, for on Frege's account we have here a name of a truth value and therefore a sentence. This is a marked departure from the doctrine of *Begriffsschrift*, according to which the place following the negation-sign can be significantly filled only by a sign whose content is a possible content of judgement;[1] the young Frege insisted on distinguishing sentences like 'Priam's house was of wood' from designations like 'Priam's house', and would have dismissed as nonsensical the replacement of 'Priam's house' even by a nominalization of a sentence like '(the circumstance of) Priam's having a house'.[2]

Dummett holds that Frege's change of mind was a regrettable error, and this time I entirely agree with Dummett. The assimilation of sentences to names made the formal logic of *Grundgesetze* run more smoothly; moreover, many of the common arguments against this assimilation are unsound. (I have argued this last matter in a paper forthcoming in *Semiotyka polska*, under the title 'Why sentences aren't names'—'Czemu zdanie nie jest nazwą'.) But all the same I think the assimilation is clearly wrong, just because sentences and names are different as regards negation: a sentence can fuse with negation to make a sentence, a name cannot fuse with negation to make a name. Even if Frege could make out '~a' to be well formed, he would be obliged to distinguish between '(~a)F' and '~(aF)': the former would be true iff the predicate 'F' were true of the object (the truth value) designated by '~a', and the latter would be true iff the predicate 'F' were *not* true of the object 'a'. It is intuitively clear that these truth conditions are quite different, and if anyone doubted this a formal proof would be easy. The contrast between this case and the happy freedom of dropping brackets in '~Fa' is very striking; and so we see once again that whereas propositions and predicates can alike be negated, names cannot.

'It's all very well to say that names have the logical properties you ascribe to them; but where can we find names in actual language?' Dummett, if I read him right, would toughly reply that we can tell something is a name from its logical behaviour: if '2' logically behaves as a name, then it is a name, and only prejudice then stops us from recognizing '2' as a name and 2 as an object. He is certainly right in criticizing my own ill-advised expression, which made it appear as if one could *first* decide that the number 2 is an object (Lord knows

[1] p. 10 of original, and p. 7 f. of Geach and Black translation.
[2] p. 2 of original and p. 2 of Geach and Black translation.

how) and *then* recognize '2' as a name. Dummett and I are further agreed that a genuine name carries with it, as part of its sense, a criterion of identity; and in this respect, as I said long ago, numerals are no worse off, raise no worse philosophical problems, than personal proper names. I have heard there are those who would regard the identity expressed by personal proper names as being conceivably non-transitive; I do not say, I do not indeed think, that this is reasonable; I merely point out that nobody has suggested non-transitive identity for whole numbers, and anyone who is willing to entertain such fancies is in no position to regard the naming role of numerals as more problematic than the naming role of personal proper names.

I am sure the reasons for thinking there could be non-transitive identity for persons are quite frivolous. A clear-headed man will not suppose that such fission or fusion as does take place, for example for amoebas and similar low organisms, affords any reason for using a non-standard logic of proper names to describe it. And if once we realize that the art of fiction writers in general and SF writers in particular enables them to cover up contradictions in the story, then we shall not have any confidence that the suppositious cases of non-transitive personal identity that are constructed are coherently described, even apart from the non-standard identity theory. So I shall here assume that 'the same human being' does give us an unequivocally transitive identity, and that this identity is expressed when we keep on using the same proper name of a human being.

Proper names of human beings are a linguistic universal; one may confidently dismiss as a tall tale or a confusion any story that some exotic language contains no such names. The fact that a name has some etymology enabling it to be adapted into English as 'Red Thunder Cloud', let us say, is not at all to the point; it is as irrelevant as the fact that a word equiform to my surname, I know not whether etymologically connected with it, figures in the Oxford English Dictionary. And once you have proper names of persons you have a means of applying the whole Fregean apparatus: for you will at once get examples of functions if you consider sentence-patterns in which now one, now another, personal name is inserted. A Chinese writer attacked the philosophical importance of the subject–predicate distinction because there was no reliable, non-arbitrary way of applying it to his own vernacular: but however that may be, his arguments could do nothing to show that the Fregean apparatus was inapplicable to Chinese, since it is quite easy to find Chinese sentences containing proper names and saying something about the persons named.

Another author, I remember, criticized a doctrine rightly maintained by Dummett, who follows the tradition of Frege and Wittgenstein: namely, that sentences consist of identifiable words, and owe their sense to the sense of those words. He gave Eskimo languages as a counter-example: an Eskimo will come out with a long string of phonemes meaning as a whole 'I am just going over to the next village to see a man about borrowing a kayak' although no separable words can be discerned in the string. How could one establish the meaning of the Eskimo sentences if this sort of thing obtained? But of course the story was a reckless untruth, as anyone could discover by looking up 'Eskimo Language' in an encyclopaedia or for that matter looking up 'kayak' in the nearest dictionary that gives etymologies. The objection would be highly relevant to the Fregean analysis, if it had had any foundation, since in a language such as Eskimo a sentence would not be a function of the names it contained; if it were so, it would be so, but as it isn't, it ain't.

I depart both from Frege and from Dummett in holding that the Fregean conception of a name is at once two narrow and too wide: too narrow, in that it excludes words for genera and species of things; too wide, in that it lets in many-worded definite descriptions. To take the second point first: I agree with Aristotle and with Wittgenstein that a name can have no significant bits; a name attaches to objects directly, not by mediation of the sense or reference of any component part. Moreover, there are every so many examples, like the following:

The woman whom every true Englishman honours above all other women is his mother,

in which the segment with the surface form 'the A that is P' cannot be treated as a syntactical unit at all, let alone as a proper name; this comes out in the paraphrase:

For every true Englishman there is just one woman whom he honours above all other women, and she is his mother.

The paraphrase in turn readily goes over into a Russellian form, in which the binding of variables corresponds to the pronoun–antecedent relation:

For every true Englishman x, there is some woman y such that x honours y and y alone above all other women, and y is x's mother.

If we pore over these examples, of which I have given many over the years and worked over many more, we ought to find that our intuition about even the syntactical coherence, let alone the namehood, of phrases like 'the woman who(m) . . .' is very slippery and unreliable, and may come to dispense with such intuitions.

The other point is more tricky. I should argue that the substitution of common nouns like 'horse' for proper names like 'Bucephalus' in principle goes over *salva congruitate*. In Polish this would certainly be so; but in English, which is cluttered with articles, you would get a Polish-sounding sentence like 'Horse which Alexander rode lived thirty years.' I do not think we need fret about these idiotisms of idiom, as Arthur Prior called them. The sentence that legend says Henryk Hiz used in a lecture on English syntax, 'In English language common noun in singular number invariably has definite or indefinite article', got its message over. Incidentally, that message is false even as regards standard English, for we say 'in the English language' but 'in English grammar', and there are many other such pairs to show the frequent logical vacuity of articles.

But do names like 'horse' satisfy my other condition of namehood —conveying a criterion of identity? They do. There is one sense of 'the same animal' in which whenever we rightly call something by the name 'Bucephalus', we are naming the same animal; there is another sense of 'the same animal' in which whenever we rightly call something by the name 'horse', we are speaking of the same animal. I consciously incur the suspicion that I am quibbling over an ambiguity; but the ambiguity is being only mentioned, not used and exploited; if I were delivering this lecture in Polish, I should render 'the same' differently, using 'ten sam' for the 'Bucephalus' case and 'taki sam' for the 'horse' case, and there would be no ambiguity to worry about.

The way we remove this ambiguity in English is inefficient and misleading, as happens with some other disambiguating devices. We disambiguate 'I'm looking for a book' by asking the question 'Do you mean a definite book?', but no classification of books into definite and indefinite ones is intended. Similarly here: people may say that it's a matter of whether we mean by 'the same animal' 'numerically the same animal' or 'the same kind of animal'; this, like the verbiage about 'a definite book', may work psychologically to get people attending to the right distinction, but it is logically unenlightening, even misleading. 'Numerically the same animal' is quite useless logically; for a count of the animals in a zoo that tags all the lions with the number 1, all the tigers with the number 2, etc., is just as much a count as a count of heads is; and by such a count any tiger is numerically the same animal as any other. The suggestions of 'the same kind of animal' are even more misleading: namely, that now we are concerned with identifying and counting not animals but more abstract objects, kinds of animals. (Quine, I fear, falls into this mistake in *Methods of Logic*.) But in English the phrase 'kind of' or 'sort of' is functionally an adjective, making up for the absence of words corresponding to Latin 'talis' and 'aliqualis', Polish 'taki' and 'jakiś' —as I said, the Polish for 'the same sort of' in this use is 'taki sam'. When I say 'She was wearing a sort of kimono' I mean that she was wearing a kimono, not a more abstract article of wear, a *sort* of kimono.

Let us get out of this blind alley. In Victorian England horse-racing men naturally knew that the Derby winner Running Rein and Maccabeus were the same animal, namely each was a horse; Lord George Bentinck discovered that they were the same animal in a stronger sense, namely the same horse. There is no question here of a relation between kinds of animals versus one between individual animals: each of the phrases, 'the same kind of animal' and 'the same individual animal', stands for an equivalence relation holding between Running Rein and Maccabeus.

But this view of the matter altogether excludes our regarding 'horse' and 'Maccabeus' as of two syntactical categories—one a proper name, the other a common name. One would normally explain the notion of a proper name thus: N is a proper name iff N names something (like Frege I exclude empty proper names from logic) and N names but one thing—if N names x and N names y then x is the same as y. But as Frege would say, 'one thing' is an expression void for uncertainty: I hold, unless we are ready to supply some definite criterion of identity, given by an equivalence relation. But if we do supply the right equivalence relation, 'horse' comes out as a proper name no less than 'Maccabeus'. Anything named by 'Maccabeus' is the same animal in the strong sense as anything named by 'Maccabeus'; but anything named by 'horse', e.g. Maccabeus, is the same animal in the weak sense as anything named by 'horse', e.g. Eclipse;

and the weak sense of 'the same animal as' still gives an equivalence relation and a criterion of identity.

I thus find myself in a position to which I have never firmly committed myself before: namely, I totally reject the distinction of syntactical category between proper names and common names. 'Horse' is a common name of Bucephalus, Maccabeus, etc., but it can also be represented as a proper name. The concept of a proper name needs to be relativized, just as identity has to be relativized: a name is not a proper name *simpliciter*, but a proper name of one and the same *A*, which does not exclude its being a common name of several *B*s. 'Horse' is a proper name of one and the same kind of animal: as I have explained, this phrase does not relate to an abstract entity, a kind of animal—the Polish words 'takiego samego zwierzęcia' would not even suggest any such thing. The difference between 'horse' and 'Bucephalus' is simply that they are names carrying with them different criteria of identity.

It might be thought that common names differ from proper names in that they can also be predicated, whereas a proper name cannot be a genuine predicate.[1] But this is a grammatical illusion. The word 'horse' in predicate position, in the context 'is a horse' (and in similar complement-constructions, e.g. 'became a horse') is not a name, and logically is not the same word as 'horse' in a logical-subject construction where 'Bucephalus' might also stand (e.g. 'Richard III's kingdom could be saved only by ——').

At this point I must try to make clear the logic of such predicates. I said long ago that I regard them as derelativizations, to use Quine's handy term. To give indisputable examples of derelativization: the two-place predicates 'is brother of', 'is sister of', 'is uncle of', cannot be regarded as formed from the one-place predicates 'is a brother', 'is a sister', 'is an uncle' by some relativizing operation: the only sensible way to describe the logic of such a pair as 'is a brother' and 'is brother of' is to regard the first as definable in terms of the second—as 'is a brother of someone or other'. I call 'is a brother' a derelativization of 'is brother of'. I hold that 'is a horse' is similarly a derelativization of 'is the same horse as', and that there is no slot for a one-place predicate in a construction 'is the same —— as' so that by slotting in '(is a) horse' we get 'is the same horse as'. Incidentally, I regard 'is the same brother as', which does after all sound a bit odd, as an ill-formed expression generated by false analogy: it could be legitimate only if 'is

[1] Cf. Frege's *On Concept and Object*, in Geach and Black's translation.

a brother' were its derelativization, or alternatively 'brother' could be slotted into 'is the same —— as'; but 'is the same —— as' is not a construction for forming relative out of non-relative terms, and 'is a brother' is a derelativization not of 'is the same brother as' but of 'is brother of'.

The truth of such sentences as 'Any horse is the same horse as something or other' does not exclude the truth that the equiform word 'horse' here has a different mode of significance at each occurrence, just as the sentence 'Snow is white' has a different mode of significance at each place in: ' "Snow is white" is true iff snow is white.' And there is no more a construction 'is the same —— as' for forming relative terms out of names than there is such a one for forming relative terms out of one-place predicates: the *name* 'horse' simply does not occur in 'is the same horse as', any more than the one-place predicate 'is an uncle' occurs in the two-place predicate 'is an uncle of'. I am of course not saying that there is no systematic connection, only that we are tempted to get it the wrong way round; the use of any name, whether vulgarly called proper or common, depends on a criterion of identity, expressed by an equivalential relative term; the equivalence relation is not expressed by some use of the name.

I add a brief note on the relation of this thought to Polish systems of 'ontology', as presented by Leśniewski and his pupils. Like them I recognize only one syntactical category of names, which includes common names like 'horse'. But there the similarity ends. They would count as names any sentence-generating fillers of the gap in, let us say, 'There is at least one, or more than one, thing which is ——'; by this criterion, 'asleep' or 'on the mat' would count as a name; such an expression, naturally, is not a name in my book, particularly in view of the manifest absurdity of regarding it as a possible subject of predication. They reject the doctrine that names must be syntactically simple. Finally, they attach a curious importance to a supposed fundamental form '*A* is *B*', whose truth will require '*A*' and '*B*' to be names that name the same thing. I regard the form as a grammatical chimera. If 'is *B*' is predicative, then it derives from 'is the same *B* as', in which, as I said, we cannot recognize any occurrence of the name '*B*'; if on the contrary 'is' means 'is the same as', this must be disambiguated to 'is the same *C* as' — '*A* is the same *C* as *B*' is then just one among many examples of the structure '*ARB*', and throws no special light on the logic of predication. We get such light only from Frege's doctrine of function and argument.

Incidentally, only lack of acquaintance with the Polish language could make people ascribe the Ontologists' love of the form '*A* is *B*' to the language most Ontologists speak. In Latin the form '*A* est *B*', with '*A*' and '*B*' free from articles and both in the nominative, is very common; in Polish the construction is rare—the language rather forces you to make up your mind which is subject and which is predicate. '*Deus erat Verbum*', 'The Word was God', does not show which noun is the predicate, but Polish 'Bogiem było Słowo' shows twice over, by the case-ending of 'Bogiem' and the grammatical concord of the copula with 'Słowo', that that is the subject, although, as in the Latin, it comes last.

The idea that common names are not logically names is a violent, and I have argued an unnecessary, departure from what vernaculars suggest: for example, by the ease of transition between proper and common names, with intermediate cases like 'I fear Cook is drunk again' said by a Victorian *materfamilias*. It is a relief to be able to return to regarding common names *as* names—though many people will have grown too stiff in the joints of thought to do this, like fanatics who keep a limb in a rigid pose. But though I am sure this move is right, it raises further problems that I know not how to solve. If I am right, not only 'Bucephalus died at thirty years of age' and 'Bucephalus did not die at thirty years of age', but also 'Horse died at thirty years of age' and 'Horse did not die at thirty years of age' will be well formed. The slight grammatical shock of this is nothing: imagine the sentences said in a Polish accent, and correct the poor devil's lack of command over the English article! But what are the truth conditions to be specified for the sentences? I am not sure, and will not inflict my half-baked thoughts on you for your consumption. Only I am sure that in the right solution 'Fa' and '$\sim Fa$' will come out as contradictories, without need of brackets, if '$F\xi$' is interpreted as 'ξ died at thirty years of age', and that whether 'a' is interpreted as 'Horse' or as 'Bucephalus'. I just cannot allow any doubt about this without destroying my criterion for namehood, for the distinction between names and predicates; and without this I no longer know what a name is, so the thesis that 'horse' is a name loses its significance.